The Image of God

Disappearing into the Divine Nature

Mark Plaiss

Paulist Press
New York/Mahwah, NJ

Cover design by Sharyn Banks
Book design by Lynn Else

Library of Congress Cataloging-in-Publication Data

Plaiss, Mark.
    The image of God : disappearing into the divine nature / Mark Plaiss.
        p. cm.
    Includes bibliographical references.
    ISBN 978-0-8091-4662-8 (alk. paper)
    1. Spirituality. 2. Spiritual life—Christianity. 3. Christian life. I. Title.
    BV4501.3.P625 2010
    248.09182′1—dc22

                                                    2009052219

Published by Paulist Press
997 Macarthur Boulevard
Mahwah, New Jersey 07430

www.paulistpress.com

Printed and bound in the
United States of America

Contents

For Adam and John, my precious sons

It is customary to blame secular science and anti-religious philosophy for the eclipse of religion in modern society. It would be more honest to blame religion for its own defeats. Religion declined not because it was refused, but because it became irrelevant, dull, oppressive, insipid. When faith is completely replaced by creed, worship by discipline, love by habit; when the crisis of today is ignored because of the splendor of the past; when faith becomes an heirloom rather than a living fountain; when religion speaks only in the name of authority rather than with the voice of compassion—its message becomes meaningless.

> Abraham Joshua Heschel
> *God in Search of Man*

This pusillanimous faith usually occurs in the form of an orthodoxy which feels threatened and is therefore more rigid than ever. It occurs wherever, in the face of the immorality of the present age, the gospel of creative love for the abandoned is replaced by the law of what is supposed to be Christian morality, and by penal law. He who is of little faith looks for support and protection for his faith, because it is preyed upon by fear. Such a faith tries to protect its "most sacred things," God, Christ, doctrine, and morality, because it clearly no longer believes that these are sufficiently powerful to maintain themselves. When the "religion of fear" finds its way into the Christian church, those who regard themselves as the most vigilant guardians of the faith do violence to faith and smother it. Instead of confidence and freedom, fearfulness and apathy are found everywhere.

Jürgen Moltmann
The Crucified God

Faith is more than the assent to dogmatic truths proposed for belief by "the authority of God revealing." It is a personal and direct acceptance of God Himself, a "receiving" of the Light of Christ in the soul, and a consequent beginning or renewal of spiritual life. But an essential element in this reception of the "light" of Christ is the *rejection* of every other "light" that can appeal to sense, passion, imagination or intellect.

Thomas Merton
The Inner Experience: Notes on Contemplation

The one accustomed to prayer only when he bends the knee prays very little.

St. John Cassian
Conferences

CHAPTER ONE

Freedom

Consider the following:

During the last thirty years there has been a tremendous defection from the Christian Church. It is evidenced even by things that lie on the surface. For example, by the decline in church attendance and in Sabbath observance and in the number of candidates for the ministry....

What is the cause of this tremendous defection?...[People] do not accept Christianity because they can no longer be convinced that Christianity is true. It may be useful, but is it true?...

I do not mean that most [people] reject Christianity consciously on account of intellectual difficulties. On the contrary, rejection of Christianity is due in the vast majority of cases simply to indifference....

But whence comes this indifference?... Modern culture is not altogether opposed to the gospel. But it is out of all connection with it. It not only prevents the acceptance of Christianity. It prevents Christianity even from getting a hearing.

This comes from an essay entitled "Christianity and Culture," published in the 1913 issue of the *Princeton Theological Review*. The author was J. Gresham Machen, a Presbyterian theologian and a faculty member of the Princeton Theological Seminary. Though published on the eve of World War I, Machen's words are just as pertinent today as they were when the Kaiser, Archduke Ferdinand, and Woodrow Wilson (a fellow Princetonian) stalked the political landscape.

Machen correctly zeroes in on the central problem Christianity faces in the West, both then and now: indifference. It is certainly true that there are people in the West who are hostile to Christianity, who harbor ill will toward it, and who mock it. From Ted Turner's pronouncement that "Christianity is a religion for losers," to MTV's comedy series *Popetown*, examples abound of derision and contempt.

The vast majority of people in the West, however, are not hostile to Christianity; they are simply indifferent to it. Both parents work, somebody has to get the kids to and from daycare and school, the weekends are filled with sports and games for the kids, and the weeknights are filled with homework for the kids and even more work from the office for the parents. Who has time for church? Christianity simply does not enter into the day-to-day routine of many, if not most, people in the West anymore. Christianity is just one other item out there, clamoring for the time and attention of the modern family.

In a story centered on the Catholic Church in Ireland published in the *Philadelphia Inquirer*, reporter David O'Reilly noted that where once there was hostility toward the Church in the eyes of young Irish people, now there is something worse in their eyes: indifference. "Basically they're saying, 'What you're offering, we don't find meaningful.'"

Humanity, however, has always been "busy." Somehow, though, it still managed to find the time to worship. Something else must be contributing to today's indifference. I believe that this something else is the modern notion of freedom.

In the West, freedom means the autonomy of the individual vis-à-vis the government as well as the Church. In regard to the Church, Westerners see dogma, doctrine, and traditions as impinging upon their freedom. Furthermore, Westerners believe that freedom is so necessary to humanity that they understand freedom as an actual "core condition" of being human. To impinge upon freedom, then, is to trample humanity.

In addition, this notion of freedom is viewed as the unimpeded ability to *choose*; that is, unimpeded in terms of statute or custom. This notion of the ability to choose has grown to such lengths as to mean the ability to choose abortion, one's own mate of either sex, or even the number of simultaneous mates. In the eyes of a growing number of people in the West, such choices are the purview of the autonomous individual, not that of the state or the Church. The level of freedom a society enjoys, then, is directly proportional to the number of choices one has. Whether or not people in the West are correct in thinking this way is not the point I am trying to make. The point is, Westerners by and large think this way.

Thus, the Church has to ask itself: How does it bring the good news to a group of people who believe that the Church is basically an infringement upon the freedom of the individual?

One way: Correct the erroneous belief that the Church is an impingement upon human freedom. After having corrected that problem, goes this theory, then catechize people that Christianity, via the Church, is the sole means to true freedom. Furthermore, this freedom will be reached only by adhering to the dogmas, doctrines, and traditions of the Church.

This approach promises a head-on collision with the culture. It attempts to overthrow the prevailing mindset by sheer intellectual force. Another problem with this course of action is that it alienates from the outset the very people it hopes to convert.

A second way desires no head-on collision with the culture in regard to the issue of freedom. This second way, instead, prefers an end-run approach: push the social dimension of Jesus. In other words, feed the poor, clothe the naked, and free the oppressed. The more people who are fed, clothed, and freed politically, the greater the number of people who will enjoy true freedom—and thus the greater the chance will be of bringing about the kingdom of God that Jesus initiated. The problem with this scenario is the danger of it morphing into merely another social-service project, with a little "Jesus loves you" thrown in to make it all appear Christian.

However, if the central issue is indeed freedom, then why not use the issue of freedom to the Church's advantage? Not as a bludgeon, as in the first way, nor by going around it as in the second way. Rather, what the Church must say to the Westerner is this: "You are right…Freedom is necessary for humanity. Let us show you how God sets you free."

The key to this approach is not stressing salvation, rules, and traditions. Doing so will only set off warning bells. Rather, the emphasis must be on the idea that freedom is not a static *thing*, but a *process* by which one grows ever more free by disappearing into the author of freedom: God.

This freedom is based on love, love of God and neighbor (Luke 10:26–28). This freedom is not static, because it evolves into holiness (2 Pet 1:4; 2 Cor 3:18; 2 Cor 5:17). Holiness is the true goal of life (1 Pet 1:15), and freedom is its springboard. The agent of this freedom and holiness is not humanity, but God (Luke 18:10–14). This holiness that is the goal of humanity and springs from true freedom, however, is stymied by something: sin. Jesus is the liberator from such sin, and it is Jesus who imbues us with true freedom.

By stressing the freedom that modern Westerners prize, the Church frees the individual from instantly measuring the Church's teaching against the individual's own standard of freedom. Once the person is set loose from that dilemma, then that individual has a much greater chance of seeing the truth of the Church's way; a much greater chance of following in the footsteps of the Lord Jesus.

Look at it this way. I don't wake up in the morning thinking, "Wow, I really feel like indulging in some adultery today. But, darn, I can't do that, because the rules say I can't. Drat!" Rather, it is: "I *love* my wife, and the thought of adultery is abhorrent, because I *love* her, and I don't want anyone or anything to come between the love she and I share." In both scenarios I am "following the rules," abiding by the commandment to not commit adultery. The second scenario, though, disengages the situation from the issue of freedom: I follow the commandment that forbids adultery, not because I'm compelled to by law, but because I love my wife. The mindset of the first scenario is basically the issue of freedom: "There is something I want to do, but some outside force is preventing me from doing what I desire to do. That is an infringement upon my freedom." The issue is freedom. The Church needs to use that issue without alienating the very people it wishes to evangelize. The answer to indifference is freedom. True freedom.

If the individual in the West today is to be converted, then he or she must see that such a conversion is to a person, Jesus Christ, not to a doctrine. Why? Because doctrine is seen as coming from beyond the individual. Doctrine is seen as being imposed from without, and that which is beyond the individual is seen as an impediment to his or her freedom.

On the other hand, conversion to a fully human, yet fully divine *person*—Jesus Christ—stands more of a chance of coming about. Why? Because an individual can more readily identify with a divine person who spoke, laughed, ate, cried, grew up, and matured. An individual can more readily identify with that person than with a set of propositions, doctrines, and dogmas. Jesus first, then catechism.

Conversion must not be reduced to mere assent to dogmatic truths. It is not that dogma should not be accepted and believed by Catholics. Rather, dogma and doctrine are not the place where conversion begins. Conversion and subsequently faith begin with an experience. In Christianity that experience is Jesus Christ.

Psalm 34:8 illustrates this point. "O taste and see that the LORD is good," says the psalmist. As Bernard of Clairvaux writes, "Unless you taste it [the sweetness of the Lord], you shall not see it. This is hidden manna, it is the new name which no one knows except him who receives it. Not learning but anointing teaches it."[1] One tastes (that is, experiences), *then* sees (that is, has knowledge). Bernard again returns to this image of tasting in Sermon 85 in his commentaries on the Song of Songs:

> When wisdom enters a soul it cuts off its appetite for evil desires, purifies the understanding and heals and restores the palate of the heart. Once its powers have been transformed in this way it starts to seek after the good things and to desire wisdom itself. There is nothing better in the whole world to do than that.[2]

Taste for wisdom, that is God, smothers the appetite for evil. When one experiences God, the desire for evil is squelched. This idea of tasting and seeing the Lord is made even more emphatic when other translations of Psalm 34:8 are used: "Taste and see that the LORD is *sweet*." Rachel Fulton notes:

Throughout the Middle Ages for the recitation of the Divine Office in the churches of the Latin West, Psalm 34:8 reads, "Taste and see that the Lord is sweet." In Jerome's AD 393 translation from the Hebrew that, with the Tridentine reforms of the sixteenth century, was to be taken up as the authoritative Vulgate version of the Roman Catholic Church, however, the same verse reads, "Taste and see that the Lord is good."[3]

When people taste the Lord—experience God—that leaves a sweet taste in their mouths; they want to go back for more. Bernard's friend William of St. Thierry knew this, too. "Then something, whatever it is—something loved rather than thought, and tasted, rather than understood—grows sweet and ravishes the lover."[4] It is precisely this taste for God that the Church must foster among the people, a taste for God, who ravishes those who love him. This taste cannot be acquired initially by doctrine, but by God alone. Once a person acquires the taste for God, the doctrine fits on the plate.

Again, the analogy of husband and wife is useful. I have been married over thirty years. I have loved my wife since I first set eyes on her in high school when she was sixteen and I was seventeen. I experienced love of her first, and I grew to believe in her. Knowledge followed experience.

Furthermore, when I experienced this love, I desired to believe. My decision to believe in the young lady who would eventually become my wife welled up from within me due to love; it was not imposed upon me from without, due to duress or argument. I chose to believe in her due to my love for her.

Likewise, the desire to believe the dogmas of the Church follow the experience of loving Jesus Christ. The rules follow the love, not the other way around. And this love of Christ? It leads to true freedom.

None of this is new. Back in the fourth century, John Cassian was saying the same thing about the person who loves Christ:

> Nor can he desire forbidden things or disdain things that are commanded, since all his concentration and longing are constantly fixed upon the divine love, and to such a degree does he not take delight in base things that he does not even make use of those things that have been conceded him. (*Conference 21*)[5]

Our first stop, then, is to witness freedom experienced through love.

CHAPTER TWO

Love

"What must I do to inherit eternal life?"

Luke 10:25

We begin with the above question, which was posed to Jesus. Variations of the question appear in all of the synoptics (Matt 22:34–40; Matt 19:16; Mark 12:28–34; Mark 10:17), but our interest here is in the Lucan formula. In the Gospel of Luke Jesus is asked this same question twice. The question is asked the first time by one who is described as "a scholar of the law." The question is asked the second time by one described as "an official." Luke 10:25 reads: "Teacher, what must I do to inherit eternal life?" Luke 18:18 reads: "Good Teacher, what must I do to inherit eternal life?" Aside from the adjective *good* in Luke 18:18, the two questions are identical.

Four assumptions lie behind this question. First, it is assumed that there is life beyond this earthly life. Furthermore, the life beyond this earthly life is deemed desirable, or else why would the scholar and the official ask how to obtain it. Third, the life that lies beyond this earthly life is believed to be everlasting. Finally, the question assumes that one can "do" something to inherit eternal life.

The question itself is a good example of the old adage: Nothing ever changes; everything remains the same. You are familiar with this exact same question; you have heard it many times. However, you know the question in its modern form: "Are you saved?" or, "What must I do to be saved?" Chances are, you have either been asked that very same question yourself, or you have heard that question asked of others. Maybe *you* have asked somebody that question. At any rate, what the official and the scholar of the Law are asking Jesus is: How can I be saved?

Two of the Matthean and Markan parallels of Luke 10:25 pose the questions differently. "Teacher, which commandment in the law is the greatest?" a scholar of the Law asks Jesus at Matthew 22:36. "Which commandment is the first of all?" a scribe asks Jesus at Mark 12:28. In Matthew and Mark the emphasis is different. In those Gospel passages, the focus is on the hierarchy of precedence within the Law of Moses. There are many commandments, but which ones are the most important? In other words, which commandment *must* be obeyed to inherit eternal life? Luke 10:25, however, addresses the issue point blank: What is necessary to have eternal life?

Jesus responds with a question of his own. "What is written in the law?" Jesus asks the scholar of the Law. Immediately, then, Jesus frames his answer within the confines of the Law. Whatever it is that is necessary to inherit eternal life, Jesus is saying, is found in the Law. The scholar of the Law replies that one shall love God and neighbor. Jesus responds, "You have given the right answer; do this, and you will live."

Note what Jesus does *not* say. In response to the scholar's question about how to inherit eternal life, Jesus does not say anything about sacrificing this or that animal; he says nothing about reciting this or that prayer *x* number of times; he says nothing about observing Passover.

Rather, Jesus concurs that the preeminent law in the Law of Moses is love…love of a *person*: God and neighbor. Not love of the Law itself, but of a person. This is not to say, however, that one should not love the Law of Moses, that one should not observe Passover. It is to say, rather, that love of God and neighbor takes precedence over love of the Law in general and over love of piety. Furthermore, if one truly loves God and neighbor, then loving the Law and observing Passover naturally falls into place.

Love of God and neighbor, then, gives one eternal life. He or she is saved who loves God and neighbor. Furthermore, such love is what the Law is all about.

Love, then, reigns supreme. St. Paul says that, in the end, when all is said and done, only three things last: faith, hope, and love. The greatest of those three, says St. Paul, is love (1 Cor 13:13). Love, then, trumps faith and is greater than hope. This makes perfect sense in light of 1 John 4:8: "God is love."

If Luke 10:25 shows the preeminence of love for God and subsequently one's neighbor, then Luke 18:18–23 spells out how that love is to be expressed. Love of God and neighbor is to be expressed by not killing, stealing, lying, or committing adultery. Love of God and neighbor is to be expressed by honoring one's mother and father. In other words, love of God and neighbor is expressed in the manner in which we deal with our neighbor and our parents.

Jesus then takes all that one step further. Not only are we to refrain from committing adultery, killing, stealing, and lying; not only are we to honor parents—we also are to follow Jesus. We are not to follow and pursue any *thing*.

Before telling the official about the Law's prohibition against adultery, murder, theft, and lies, however, Jesus makes an interesting little comment; an interjection, really, that can easily be dismissed as just a throwaway line. Jesus says: "You know the commandments" (Luke 18:20).

The official already *knows* those prohibitions. Presumably, that official also observes those same prohibitions. But doing so is not enough to inherit eternal life. Knowledge and observance of the Law are not enough. If knowledge and observance of the Law were enough, then in the parable of the Pharisee and the tax collector, the Pharisee would have gone home justified (Luke 18:9–14). No, one must follow Jesus as well.

So it is not what you know; it is who you love. Furthermore, love gives one the desire and strength to follow the beloved. Thus, to love and to follow are opposite sides of the same coin called faith. We follow Jesus because we love him; we uphold the commandments because we love God and because we don't want to separate ourselves from God by committing evil. I, as a married man, do not commit adultery, simply because the rules (the commandments) say I cannot. Rather, I do not engage in adultery because I love my wife, and it is that love that gives me the desire and strength to obey the commandment that prohibits adultery.

When Jesus tells the official to follow him (Luke 18:23), the official grows sad. The pericope is silent on whether or not the official accepts Jesus' challenge to sell all his goods and to follow Jesus, but the implication is that the official does neither. That saddens Jesus.

Why? Why would that sadden Jesus? After all, the official has observed the Law: He has not committed adultery. He has not killed, stolen, or lied. He has honored his mother and father. What is more, the official has observed this Law since his youth. He has abided by all the rules. Isn't that good enough?

Again, simple observation of the Law is not enough. One must also follow Jesus.

How frequently have you heard someone say in regard to his or her own virtue: "It's not like I've killed anybody!" And of course, that is good. It is also good that one does not engage in adultery, theft, or lies. Those are certainly things to avoid.

But the question of inheriting eternal life, as asked by the official at Luke 18:18, is not completely answered by just refraining from killing, lying, stealing, and from being adulterous. Any human being, Christian or not, can refrain from adultery, killing, stealing, and lying. Any human being, of any religion, can love his or her parents.

Near the end of John's Gospel, Jesus asks Peter three times if he loves *him* (John 21:15–17). Jesus does not ask Peter if he loves the *works* he has performed. Nor does Jesus ask Peter if he loves the *idea* of turning the other cheek or loving one's enemies. No, Jesus asks Peter if he loves *him*, Jesus. Note, too, that when Jesus asks him this same question three times, Jesus addresses Peter by his given name, Simon. In the same way, Jesus calls each of us by name; Jesus asks each of us, by name, if we love him. Then, at the end of that pericope in John, Jesus tells Peter to follow him. Love produces the desire to follow. One freely follows a person one loves.

Eternal life is gained by loving God and neighbor, and by following Jesus. But that brings up another question: How does one follow Jesus?

CHAPTER THREE

The Way

"I am the way and the truth and the life. No one comes to the Father except through me."

John 14:6

The ways in which someone comes to the Father through Jesus vary. Jesus gives no hint as to what those various ways may be. The trouble is, Christianity has traditionally assumed that one comes to the Father through explicit faith in Jesus. Note that Jesus says nothing about that. True, Jesus says, "Believe also in me" (John 14:1), but the context there is different. There, Jesus is trying to show the disciples the relationship between himself and the Father. At John 14:6, however, Jesus is saying that access to the Father is through him; he says nothing there, though, about access to the Father being determined by explicit faith in him. Jesus simply says that access to the Father is *through* him. To assume Jesus means that explicit faith in him gains access to the Father is to go beyond what the text says and to drift off into mere speculation.

Furthermore, the emphasis in 14:6 is not on Jesus, the *me* of the pericope. Rather, the emphasis is on the *Father*. That is why Jesus says in John 14:2 that there are many dwelling places in his Father's house. Jesus does not say there are many dwelling places in *his* house. The goal is the Father, and Jesus is the way to that goal. Hence, Philip's question: "Lord, show us the Father, and we will be satisfied" (John 14:8).

But Jesus, so close to the Father, can confidently and truly reply: "Whoever has seen me has seen the Father" (John 14:9). In fact, their relationship is so close that Jesus can proclaim, "The Father and I are one" (John 10:30). Jesus is what the Father looks like in human form. However, Jesus does not exhaust the person of the Father; the divinity of God transcends the humanness of Jesus of Nazareth. Thus, despite this closeness between Jesus and the Father, Jesus can still insist, "The Father is greater than I" (John 14:28).

If the ways in which one comes to the Father through Jesus vary, what could some of those ways be? Could they be through other religious traditions?

On May 19, 1991, the Pontifical Council for Interreligious Dialogue, then headed by Francis

Cardinal Arinze, issued a document entitled "Dialogue and Proclamation: Reflections and Orientations on Interreligious Dialogue and the Proclamation of the Gospel of Jesus Christ." This document was approved for promulgation by Pope John Paul II. Paragraph twenty-nine of that document says this:

> It will be in the sincere practice of what is good *in their own religious traditions* and by following the dictates *of their conscience* that members of other religions respond positively to God's invitation and receive salvation in Jesus Christ, even while *they do not recognize or acknowledge him as their savior* [emphasis mine].

Furthermore, in his 1990 encyclical *Redemptoris Missio*, Pope John Paul II wrote, "Although participated forms of mediation of different kinds and degrees are not excluded, they acquire meaning and value *only* from Christ's own mediation, and they cannot be understood as parallel or complimentary to his" [par. 5, emphasis in the original]. Still, Pope John Paul acknowledged the existence of mediation between God and humanity in other religions *insofar* as such mediation derives its efficacy from its association with Jesus Christ.

To be sure, the salvific efficacy of the other religious traditions stems not from those religion per se, but from *Jesus Christ*. Yet, the manner in which that salvation is concretely practiced can be through other religious traditions. Thus, the followers of other religions come to the Father through Jesus Christ, but not with explicit faith in Jesus. Though the manner is different, those persons from other religions still come to the Father through Jesus Christ, even if—as "Dialogue and Proclamation" states—those persons do not recognize or acknowledge Jesus as savior.

Let me be clear. Jesus Christ is true God and true man. Jesus Christ is the sole mediator between God and humanity (1 Tim 2:5).

Humanity as a whole, and individual persons in particular, find salvation from everlasting death *only* in the birth, life, death on the cross, and resurrection from the dead of Jesus Christ. Any salvific efficacy found in religions other than Christianity is due only to Jesus Christ, in some mysterious manner known only to God. Furthermore, the Holy Roman Church is the normative way such mediation and salvation are carried out in human history since the time of Jesus Christ. However, the Holy Roman Church, as evidenced by such Church documents as "Dialogue and Proclamation" and *Redemptoris Missio*, does not exhaust the manner of Christ's salvation.

Jacques Dupuis, a Jesuit priest born in Belgium but who spent much of his priestly career in India, wrote an interesting book entitled *Christianity and the Religions: From Confrontation to Dialogue.* In the first chapter of that book Dupuis writes:

> John's Gospel has Jesus say: "I am the way, and the truth, and the life. No one comes to the Father except through me." The mediation of Jesus Christ as "the way" to the Father does not mean that other religious traditions cannot offer their adherents "paths" of salvation through which the constitutive way of Jesus Christ might be operative, albeit in secret and imperfectly; nor that the founders and saving figures of other religious traditions cannot serve in an unconscious and incomplete way as "pointers" toward the salvation realized in him who is personally constituted by God as the only way to him. Christ's sole mediation does not stand in the way of "participated mediations" present and operative in other traditions, which derive their meaning and their saving power from Christ.[1]

In an earlier book Dupuis was even more blunt:

> To say that Christ is at the center of the divine plan for humanity is not to consider him as the goal and end toward which the religious life of human beings and the religious traditions of humanity tend. God (the

Father) remains the goal and end. Jesus never replaces God. Jesus Christ is at the center of the mystery as obligatory Mediator, constituted by God and no one else, as the way leading to God. Jesus Christ is at the center because God, not human beings or Christianity, has placed him there.[2]

So what does it mean to follow Jesus? For people in other religious traditions, following Jesus might mean not *consciously* following Jesus at all. Simply loving God above all things and loving neighbor as oneself can mean following Jesus.

We have seen that Scripture and Tradition both attest to everlasting life for persons beyond the confines of the Holy Roman Church, the normative vehicle in this world to everlasting life. Let us now take a closer look at an example of this idea—of "outsiders" in fact being "insiders"—by none other than Jesus himself.

CHAPTER FOUR

Us/Them

"Sir, even the dogs under the table eat the children's crumbs."

Mark 7:28

I n Mark 7:24–30, Jesus heals the daughter of a Syrophoenician woman, even though neither the daughter nor the Syrophoenician woman herself follows Jesus, acknowledges his teachings, or professes faith in him.

Jesus, who has been trying to avoid crowds, attempts to lay low in a house in the district of Tyre, which is in modern-day Lebanon. His plan for privacy is foiled, however, by a woman Mark calls "a Gentile, of Syrophoenician origin." This woman approaches Jesus, falls at his feet, and asks him to heal her daughter who is possessed by a demon. Jesus, perhaps miffed at being discovered after trying so hard to remain hidden, dismisses the woman's request.

It is the manner in which he dismisses her request that startles the reader. Says Jesus: "Let the children be fed first, for it is not fair to take the children's food and throw it to the dogs" (Mark 7:27). The parallelism in that sentence is jarring. If the "children" are the Jews, then the "dogs" must be Gentiles, in this case the Syrophoenician woman and her daughter. This is clearly an insult. As Joseph Klausner notes, "If any other Jewish teacher of the time had said such a thing Christians would never have forgiven Judaism for it."[1]

Though the woman's hopes for her daughter's being healed are seemingly dashed, she turns the table on Jesus with her pithy retort: "Sir, even the dogs under the table eat the children's crumbs" (Mark 7:28). This witticism, the punch line to the story, turns Jesus' metaphor of children and dogs to her advantage. She acknowledges her station in life ("dogs"), but acknowledges as well that even dogs must eat, if only crumbs.

Jesus relents. "For saying that, you may go," he says to the woman. "The demon has left your daughter" (Mark 7:29).

To what does *that* refer? John Donahue and Daniel Harrington argue that the Greek means literally "because of your word."[2] Joel Marcus concurs.[3] Thus, Jesus excuses the woman and grants her request on the basis of her *words*. Faith, it seems, is not a factor in Jesus' miraculous cure of the woman's daughter. This flies in the face of episodes of healing at Mark 2:5, 5:34, and 10:52 where Jesus explicitly says that faith is the key factor. Indeed, the Matthean parallel to our Markan pericope notes this vexing predicament, and in that version of the story, Matthew "fixes" the predicament by having Jesus say to the woman, "Woman, great is your faith! Let it be done for you as you wish" (Matt 15:28). Here in Mark, however, Jesus appears to have realized he was bested in a battle of wits and has acquiesced.

Could the *that* of verse 29 refer to faith expressed *indirectly* by the woman? I think not. If Mark had believed that faith were the key issue in the healing of the woman's daughter, Mark would have placed the word *faith* on the lips of Jesus just as Mark did at 2:5, 5:34, and 10:52. As Robert Gundry points out, "Nowhere does Mark's text [in this passage] identify the moment of faith or even mention faith—only cleverness in pressing the request."[4]

Furthermore, any exegesis of this pericope that strives to lessen the severity of Jesus' actions and words is misguided. The text supports no evidence that Jesus did not really mean what he said, that he was "really" only "testing" the Syrophoenician woman. Jesus meant what he said.

This episode is frequently referred to as the story of the Syrophoenician woman. That title is a misnomer, however, for the story is not about the Syrophoenician woman (whose name is never mentioned), but about Jesus. If Luke is to be taken at his word—"and Jesus increased in wisdom" (2:52)—then this pericope in Mark is a clear example of Jesus increasing in wisdom.

Remember, this story takes place in Gentile territory. Jesus is not on his home turf (Galilee) nor in the vicinity of Jerusalem. In other words, *Jesus* is the foreigner in this story, not the Syrophoenician woman. As a foreigner, Jesus' eyes are opened to "the other," and his sparring with this woman is the catalyst that opens his eyes.

This pericope tackles the issue of exclusivist identity: Who is in and who is out? Here Jesus comes to see that those "outside" (for example, such as the likes of the Syrophoenician woman) can also be those "inside" (the kingdom of God).

This problem of exclusivist identity was already raised in the previous pericope at 7:1–23. There, it is Jesus who confronts those who seek to limit or restrict proper religious observance (Pharisees and scribes). The Pharisees ask Jesus how it is that he and his disciples do not "live according to the tradition of the elders, but eat with defiled hands" (Mark 7:5). Jesus replies that "there is nothing outside a person that by going in can defile" (Mark 7:15). Within Judaism, Jesus is telling the Pharisees, there is no demarcation between "clean" and "unclean" in regard to ritual cleansing of the hands; there is no exclusivist identity, there is no "outside": All the Jews are "inside."

However, in verses 24–30—the story of the Syrophoenician woman—the tables are turned. Here, *Jesus* is put on the spot regarding the issue of exclusivist identity, and he is put on the spot, not by a fellow Jew, but by a nonbelieving Gentile. In verses 1–23 the debate is intra-Jewish; here, the debate is Jewish-Gentile, and the Gentile is a woman. The reader of Mark just saw Jesus explain to the Pharisees in verses 1–23 that among Jews there is no group that is "outside": All the Jews are inside.

Here, however, Jesus' presumption that non-Jews are "outside" is challenged; challenged by a Gentile. That the two stories are adjacent is hardly coincidental. Taken as a whole, Mark 7:1–30 shows that the boundaries between clean and unclean, Jew and Gentile, are artificial, manmade, and not of God. At Mark 8:21, Jesus asks his disciples, "Do you not yet understand?" Here, at Mark 7:24–30, the Syrophoenician woman understands, and thanks to her so does Jesus.

There is no "them" and "us." There is only "us." Freedom consists in part in understanding that there is no "other." The law that supposedly upholds the dichotomy between "them" and "us" does not exist.

CHAPTER FIVE

Mercy

"For all who exalt themselves will be humbled."
Luke 18:14

Two people, we are told, go up to the Temple area to pray. One person is a Pharisee, the other is a tax collector.

The Pharisee begins his prayer. It is a prayer of thanksgiving. Yet, the Pharisee gives thanks not for any gifts or blessings bestowed on him by God, but rather for what he —the Pharisee—is not; he is not greedy, dishonest, or adulterous. Then the Pharisee mentions the tax collector in his prayer, and his tone is smug. He quickly goes on to mention that he fasts twice per week and tithes on his entire income.

Such activity is beyond what was required. Jews were required to fast only one day per year, on the Day of Atonement (Lev 16:29–31; Num 29:7). As for tithing, Deuteronomy 14:22–28 proscribes tithes on produce of the land. The Pharisee of this parable, however, tithes his entire income, not simply a portion of his income. So just as in regard to fasting, the Pharisee exceeds the demands of the Law in regard to tithing. Aside from the disparaging remark about the tax collector, then, the Pharisee's catalog of piety is admirable. He gives thanks for not being greedy, dishonest, or adulterous—assuredly good things not to be. Furthermore, fasting and tithing are good and admirable practices.

The problem, though, is not the piety of the Pharisee; the problem is that which motivates him. The sin of the Pharisee is neither arrogance nor moral superiority. Rather, the sin of the Pharisee is idolatry. He worships himself. The Pharisee's words as spoken in the Temple are not a prayer, but a boast. Though he pays lip service to God, the Pharisee really sees himself, not God, as the agent of holiness that works within him. The Pharisee betrays his idolatry most egregiously when he says, "I thank you [God] that I am not like the *rest of humanity*." All of humanity—God's creation—is flawed save himself. Then, in verse 12, the Pharisee relates how and why he himself is not flawed: "*I* fast" and "*I* give a tenth of all my income." He is the agent of his own holiness.

The scene turns to the tax collector. It is safe to say that tax collectors were a despised lot during the time of Jesus. They were Jews who collected taxes for the occupiers of the Jews: the Romans. In the process of collecting taxes for the hated Romans, these Jewish tax collectors extorted even more money from their fellow Jews for themselves.

Verse 13 tells us that the tax collector was "standing far off." From the distant precincts of the Temple, then, the tax collector begins his prayer. While the man prays, we are told, he would not even raise his eyes to heaven.

He speaks one line, a paraphrase of Psalm 51. The prayer is one of petition, asking for mercy. The tax collector is contrite, but is he repentant? Restitution of extorted money would be a component of any repentance of the sins for which he is contrite. Yet, nothing in the tax collector's words or actions suggest he will make restitution or even mend his ways. However, as William Herzog points out, it would be next to impossible for the tax collector to even identify his marks, let alone be able to repay the money extorted.[1] Furthermore, as Jeremias writes, an added five percent of the ill-gotten gains would also have to be tacked on.[2] There is no hint at all, here, of reparations as with Zacchaeus at Luke 19:1–9. Finally, F. Gerald Downing stresses that the original hearers of this parable may very well have scoffed at the tax collector's meek and awkward plea for mercy. Writes Downing, "What kind of deity would insist on being placated thus? So nervous a response, so lacking in trust that the speaker dared not even look up, would be nothing short of insulting."[3] Presumably, the tax collector knows all this, and the burden of his guilt and the knowledge of his inability to repay weighs heavily upon him. Hence, he feels even more isolated.

So the scene is thus: A man from a well-respected strata of Jewish religiosity, a Pharisee, gives thanks to God in the Temple at Jerusalem. This Pharisee does all the right and lawful things, but the odor of self-aggrandizement wafts about him. At the same time and in the same place a despised person instantly tagged as a sinner—a tax collector—begs God for mercy. However, this tax collector makes no mention of mending his ways or of making restitution.

In a verdict that many first hearers of this parable would undoubtedly have found surprising, Jesus proclaims the tax collector justified. Why? The answer lies in the question posed at the parable that immediately precedes this one.

The parable of the persistent widow comes immediately before the parable of the Pharisee and the tax collector. At the conclusion of the persistent widow parable is the question: "And yet, when the Son of Man comes, will he find faith on earth?" (Luke 18:8). The contention here is that the parable of the Pharisee and the tax collector is a description of the level of faith that will be found on earth at the coming of the Son of Man. In other words, the parable of the Pharisee and the tax collector is the answer to Jesus' own question posed at the conclusion of the previous parable. That contention is clearer if one reads the two parables together. In such a reading, the question is asked in verse 8, and the parable of the Pharisee and the tax collector becomes an expanded answer, complete with an illustration, to the question posed at verse 8.

What does the second pericope illustrate? At the heart of this parable is not the issue of prayer, but of mercy. Prayer is merely the outward manifestation of the faith that is being illustrated in the parable. In the Pharisee we see faith with all of its visible, outward properties. He is careful to observe and even exceed all that is required of him. We see piety. The Pharisee makes a fatal error, however. He concludes that it is his observance of the Law, even his exceeding the Law's requirements, that justifies him. He is banking on his piety. His faith is not in God, but in himself. The Pharisee betrays his ignorance of true faith as illustrated in Psalm 65:2–3:

> To you all flesh shall come.
> When deeds of iniquity overwhelm us,
>   you forgive our transgressions.

The Pharisee forgives himself simply by virtue of his own actions. No doubt, the Pharisee believes in the God of Abraham, Isaac, and Jacob, but the Pharisee also believes that the agent of his holiness is himself. Piety wins the day.

The tax collector, on the other hand, is cognizant of two things: He is a sinner, and the agent of any holiness he may wish to possess will certainly come from God, not from him. Hence, the punch line of the parable at verse 14a proclaims the tax collector justified.

However, a problem remains. How much faith does the tax collector actually have? True, he has thrown himself on the mercy of God, and that certainly is a start. However, will that spark of faith he exhibited by his outward contrition (standing back, beating his breast, looking down) deepen? The tax collector obviously takes to heart the passage in Psalm 65, but how about his observance of the Law? Will he ever approach the level of observance as exhibited by the Pharisee?

In essence, then, both the Pharisee and the tax collector are incomplete in regard to faith. Both men show signs of faith, but cannot or never will, reach a level of true faith. One shows all the outward signs of having it, but rings hollow inside. The other man obviously possesses the seeds of deep faith, but seems to have no means to make those seeds grow.

That is exactly the point of this parable. When the Son of Man returns, he will find people whose faith will be partial, incomplete. Bernard Brandon Scott is correct: The hearer of this parable "cannot imitate the behavior of one or the other" of these men.[4] Again, though, that is the point of this parable:

God's mercy will prove greater than the inadequacy of human faith. The key here is the image posed at the end of the parable of the persistent widow: "when the Son of Man *comes* (Luke 18:8). Note that the emphasis is on God coming to humanity, not vice versa. In this light, the parable of the Pharisee and the tax collector fits in well with the three parables in Luke 15 where God is searching, finding, and rejoicing.[5] In those parables at Luke 15, the lost sheep does not "deserve" to be found, nor does the lost coin. Furthermore, the younger son does not deserve the largess of the father. Yet, shower his younger son with love and gifts the father does. In the same way, when the Son of Man returns, God's mercy will prove greater than the partial and incomplete faith of the Pharisee and the tax collector.

Both the Pharisee and the tax collector in this parable want for faith. But that is exactly what the parable points out: that when the Son of Man returns, he will find faith that is only partial at best. The fact that the tax collector returned home justified, while the Pharisee did not return home justified—but not damned, by the way—does not distract from this view. Rather, we merely learn that upon the coming of the Son of Man, he will find the justified as well as the unjustified. In either event, however, the mercy of God will prove greater than any degree of faith found in humanity, whether found in the justified or the unjustified. (But not the damned—again, no mention is made in the parable that the Pharisee is damned.)

A core issue with both men of this parable is that of holiness. The Pharisee fails to acknowledge that the agent of holiness is God. He may very well believe, intellectually, that God is the source of all holiness, but his actions and demeanor as portrayed in this parable suggest otherwise. Instead, the Pharisee is content to rely on piety to justify himself. Piety is fine, except when it is used as a bludgeon to enter the realm of the sacred.

This is exactly the Pharisee's problem. Since he at heart believes that he is the agent of his own holiness, he uses piety to enter into the realm of the sacred. Just the opposite is true, however. The truly pious person exercises piety *not* in order to enter into the sacred; rather, the pious person exercises piety in order that the sacred might *enter into him or her*. The difference is one of kind, not degree. The truly pious person detests show.

Furthermore, true piety craves the transcendent. "O God, you are my God, I seek you, my soul thirsts for you" (Psalm 63:1). Yet, one does not sense the Pharisee of this parable longing for God at all. Rather, one senses the Pharisee as perfectly satisfied with his piety. He is just fine with his fasting and tithing. He very much resembles the sinner mentioned in Psalm 36:1–2: "There is no fear of God before their eyes. For they flatter themselves in their own eyes, that their iniquity cannot be found out and hated." The Pharisee's attempt to smash through into the realm of the sacred fails, and hence he returns home unjustified. The irony, of course, is that his attempt to smash through to the realm of the sacred is carried out in the holiest and most sacred place in all Judaism: the Temple.

The tax collector, loathsome as he would have been to the first hearers of this parable, at least realizes that he himself lacks any means to create his own holiness. That, he knows, must come from God. The tax collector is void of any piety except the most basic: humility. Unlike the Pharisee, the tax collector brings nothing to the Temple save contrition. Also, unlike the Pharisee, the tax collector has absolutely no good works to offer God in reparation for his sins.

The tax collector, in a sense, is completely naked before God. He is dependent upon God for God's mercy, for this tax collector—unlike the Pharisee—has no piety nor good works on which to rest his laurels. It is in this very dependence that the tax collector has upon God, and in the tax collector's acknowledgment of that dependence, that he returns home justified. It is that acknowledgment of his need for God's mercy, and his sincere request for it, that bestows holiness upon the tax collector.

Again, the irony. The person who enters the Temple with absolutely nothing in hand to sacrifice to God in reparation for his sins leaves the Temple justified. The echo of Hosea 5:15 is quite strong here: "I will return again to my place until they acknowledge their guilt and seek my face." The tax collector, unlike the Pharisee, seeks God's face.

Yet, has the tax collector paid for his guilt? As we have seen, that would be nearly impossible for him to do. The strength of this parable lies in the acknowledgment that both men are, in the end, found wanting, and that it is only God's mercy that will overcome their respective shortcomings.

No them. No us. Just mercy...and freedom.

CHAPTER SIX

Salvation

All of us, with unveiled faces, seeing the glory of
the Lord as though reflected in a mirror, are being
transformed into the same image from one degree
of glory to another; for this comes from the Lord,
the Spirit.

2 Corinthians 3:18

So far we have seen that freedom is rooted in
love, and that freedom is the springboard to
holiness. In the previous chapter, we saw that
we human beings do not produce holiness, that
holiness comes from God. How, then, do we human
beings receive holiness?

Before we can answer that, we must first understand what holiness is.

Many modern-day Westerners cringe at the
mention of "salvation." They cringe because salvation is seen as some "thing" beyond the individual,

which impinges upon their freedom. Again, Westerners may be incorrect in thinking that way, but the reality is, that is the way in which Westerners by and large think.

So, what if the Church were not to stress the word *salvation*, but instead were to stress the idea of *holiness*? This is not to say, of course, that the Church should not be concerned with the salvation of souls. Rather, it is to say that in order for the Church today to be concerned with the salvation of souls, the terminology used for the idea of salvation should change. Recall the words of John XXIII at the opening of Vatican II: "The substance of the ancient doctrine of the deposit of faith is one thing, and the way in which it is presented is another."[1] Likewise, salvation is one thing, but the way we explain it is quite another.

Benedict XVI has said as much as well. On his 2008 trip to the United States, Benedict said, "It is becoming more and more difficult, in our Western societies, to speak in a meaningful way of 'salvation'....We need to discover new and engaging ways of proclaiming this message."[2]

So let us present the ancient doctrine of salvation in terms more palatable for modern people:

Salvation is about being holy. Holiness is all about transforming more and more into the likeness of God, a process called *theosis*. Holiness is nothing other than sharing in the divine nature (2 Pet 1:4) as we—believers in Christ—are transformed into his image (2 Cor 3:18).

However, this transformation into holiness, this theosis, is not of one's own doing. Rather, this transformation is initiated and kept in progress by the loving action of God through the Church. Humans respond to this invitation to transform into the likeness of God; they are in no way the agent of this transformation.

Humans respond by allowing themselves to be molded into God's image. Allowing this is not purely passive, however. Allowing this is participating with God through prayer and love of neighbor, and it is this prayer and love of neighbor—initiated and sustained by God—that transforms humans into the image of God. Of course, humans have the ability to choose not to respond to God's invitation of transformation. This ongoing choice to refuse God's invitation is called sin, and the ultimate refusal of God's invitation to transform into the image and likeness of God is called death.

The church fathers clearly understood this transformation into the image of God. In his commentary on the Second Letter to the Corinthians, Cyril of Alexander writes: "The light of the Only-Begotten has shone on us, and we have been transformed into the Word, the source of all life."[3] And this from Gregory of Nyssa:

Take a piece of iron as an illustration. Although it might have been black before, once the rust has been scraped off with a whetstone, it will begin to shine brilliantly and to reflect the rays of the sun. So it is with the interior man, which is what the Lord means by the heart. Once a man removes from his soul the coating of filth that has formed on it through his sinful neglect, he will regain his likeness to his Archetype, and be good. For what resembles the supreme Good is itself good. If he looks into himself, he will see the vision he has longed for.[4]

This transformation is a lifelong process. One does not wake up on Tuesday morning and say to oneself: "You know, nothing is going on today...I think I'll transform myself into the likeness of God." Transformation takes time: "For you need endurance, so that when you have done the will of God, you may receive what was promised" (Heb 10:36). Furthermore, one can never be fully and completely transformed. There are only degrees of transformation. Since transformation is essentially love, and since love is limitless, one can never reach the limit of transformation. One does not wake up one morning and say to his or her spouse: "Well, Hon, I've reached the limit of my love for you. I can love you no more than I can right now.

That's it." Similarly, transformation into the likeness of God can never be exhausted, because God is inexhaustible.

Allowing ourselves to be transformed into the likeness of God, holiness, is the fuel that drives us to do good. When I am transformed into the likeness of God, I desire to do good. I want to please my beloved, who is God.

> How fair and pleasant you are,
>> O loved one, delectable maiden!
> You are stately as a palm tree,
>> and your breasts are like its clusters.
> I say I will climb the palm tree,
>> and lay hold of its branches.
> Oh, may your breasts be like clusters of the
>>> vine,
>> and the sent of your breath like apples,
> and your kisses like the best wine.
>> (Song 7:7–10)

Love, then, not only attracts, but it also impels one to "climb the palm tree," to do something for the beloved: good deeds.

The trouble is that many, if not most, Christians see it the opposite way. They do good things in order to try to get close to God. But as St. Paul notes, "We are...created in Christ Jesus for good works" (Eph 2:10). We are not created *for* good works in order to reach Jesus. That route is doomed to frustration. It is doomed to frustration, because the doing of good deeds will always be seen as a duty, as an obligation. I am here, and God is there, and I will attempt to bridge that gap between us by doing good deeds. Then God will have to love me, or at least let me into heaven, because I've done all these good things. This is "Christianity as contract."

But it is by being transformed into the likeness of God that we do good things. When I am transformed into the likeness of Christ, there is no distance between humanity and God. God and I are close. Good deeds are then not the result of duty or obligation, but the fruit of love. Christianity is no longer a contract, but a love affair.

Mary is the perfect model for this transformation into holiness. Mary's greatness, the reason all generations call her blessed, is because she was always radically open to God, always radically ready to do God's will. At the wedding feast at Cana, Mary points to her son Jesus and tells those there, "Do whatever he tells you" (John 2:5). Mary always did the same, and she did so not from a sense of obligation, but out of love.

The Holy Spirit brings about this transformation to holiness, and this transformation is salvation. Salvation is the process of being transformed into the likeness of Christ, which is holiness. Salvation, therefore, is not in its essence juridical. Merton puts this plainly and succinctly:

If the Son of Man came to seek and to save that which was lost, this was not merely in order to reestablish man in a favorable juridical position with regard to God; it was to elevate, change and transform man into God in order that God might be revealed in Man, and that all men might become One Son of God in Christ.[5]

Merton, though, is swimming against the current of today's thought that prevails in Christianity in regard to salvation. Robert Daly, quoting Stephen Finlan, succinctly puts the issue of salvation—as it is conceived in the minds of most Christians—into neat points:

...traditional Western atonement theory includes or is ultimately reducible to: (1) God's honor was damaged by human sin; (2) God demanded a bloody victim—innocent or guilty—to pay for human sin; (3) God was persuaded to alter the divine verdict against humanity when the Son of God offered to endure humanity's punishment; (4) the death of the Son thus functioned as a payoff; salvation was purchased.

Then Daly's punch line: "If this, or this kind of, atonement theory is central to our idea of God and of salvation, we are in deep trouble."[6]

45

The trouble is that for many Christians, both Protestant and Catholic, the juridical model is the only valid model, and perhaps the only one ever known. This is not to say that the juridical model is wrong. It is to say, though, that the juridical model is ineffective vis-à-vis today's society, a society that Christians are called to evangelize.

Furthermore, this distaste for the juridical approach to salvation is not something unique to post–World War II Christians. Charles Taylor sees discomfort with this approach going back several centuries:

> What made Christianity particularly repulsive to the Enlightenment mind was the whole juridical-penal way in which the doctrine of original sin and the atonement were cast during the high middle ages and the Reformation. Our distance from perfection was glossed as just punishment for earlier sin and our salvation through Christ as his offering satisfaction for this fault, paying the fine, as it were.[7]

The Church would be wise to stress transformation into the likeness of God, which is salvation, which is holiness. So how do we go about this process of transformation, this salvation that is called holiness? We go about it through prayer.

CHAPTER SEVEN

Image

So God created humankind in his image,
   in the image of God he created them;
   male and female he created them.

Genesis 1:27

Prayer begins with image. Humanity is the apex of creation, because humanity is created in the image of God. Mark Twain's quip that "man is the only animal that blushes—or needs to," is not only funny, but also accurate. Humanity blushes when it betrays the image in which it is created, and of all creation only humanity possesses the divine image. Hence, only humanity blushes.

The image of God is freedom and love. Freedom is not to be confused with license. License serves whim and compulsion, while authentic freedom is the servant of love. Freedom rises above license and is able to withstand the onslaught of desires that curtail freedom. Freedom is capable of rising above license, because of love. Love fuels freedom, and freedom drives love toward its natural end: God. Since God is love (1 John 4:16), and since my existence depends on God, then love is the reason for my existence. To love God with all my heart, soul, mind, and strength (Mark 12:30) is not just the greatest of the commandments, it is the very purpose of my life. I am created in order to love God. My neighbor is also the image of God, so I am to love my neighbor for no other reason than that neighbor is God's image.

It is the nature of humanity to love God. Original sin, however, has maimed humanity's inclination to love God. Instead, humanity tends to spurn love of God for love of self. Priorities become reversed, and the image within humanity becomes tarnished. Sin is failure to reflect the image of God. Through sin I reject not just God, but myself as well. I throw away my true self for a false self. The false self is the self that has been developed in my own likeness rather than in the likeness of God. The logical conclusion to sin is death (Rom 6:23), which is nothing more than the extinction of the image in the person, the complete absence of freedom and love. This extinction does not come from God; it is the choice of the person (Sir 15:17). Death is the expiration of both the body and the soul. When we attend the funeral of a loved one, a believer, a person stamped with the image of God, we mourn and weep. But that person is not dead; that person lives. Only the mode of existence has changed. The image of God trumps the death of the body.

The degree to which humanity is maimed is so great that humanity is unable on its own to restore the image that is natural to it. Only the grace of God can restore the image. God does so not by remaining the creator of the image, but by becoming the creature that receives it.

Jesus of Nazareth is the incarnation of the image (Col 1:15). In Jesus dwells not just the fullness of deity, but also the fullness of humanity. Jesus is what humanity is supposed to be. Through the incarnation, God simply does not tell us what we are, he *shows* us what we are. The incarnation, then, begets a totally new union between God and humanity; the incarnation is a new covenant with humanity. In this covenant God does not tell, he shows; he is not distant, but near; he is not inanimate, but flesh and blood.

To relegate Jesus, then, to the level of an enlightened philosopher or a moral leader, as some intellectuals strive to do, is to completely miss the point. God could create any number of prophets of great moral fiber and philosophical acumen, and indeed God has done so. But in Jesus of Nazareth, God has done something radical: God takes on flesh. By embracing our humanity, God realigns the relationship between Creator and creation. No longer will the relationship revolve around: "I will be your God and you shall be my people." Instead, the relationship is: "I will be your God and I shall live among you" (Matt 1:23; 28:20). Christ, God incarnate, restores the tarnished image by becoming one of us.

On the other hand, to elevate Jesus of Nazareth to divinity only, as some Christians do, is to strip the incarnation of meaning. God could very well have come to us as God Almighty, set things right, then demanded obedience and praise. To do so, however, would have solved nothing. The image of God needs to be restored; humanity's freedom and love need to once more shine. Jesus of Nazareth, the Christ, accomplishes that in his very person by becoming one of us.

Through Christ we become a new creation; "new" in the sense that Christ has made us what we were created to be in the first place. This renewal in Christ affects not just the relationship between myself and God. This renewal affects my relationship between myself and all of humanity. Humanity becomes my brother and sister, because they are my siblings in the image of God. Love and mercy are the order of the day when I interact with the image, for the person who has received God's love must in turn show that love to others. This love is greater than faith, greater than hope (1 Cor 13:13; Col 3:14), for love is the essence of God. As God loves me, so I must love my brothers and sisters. What has God given me by creating me in his image, and what has Christ given me in restoring that image? Love. Love is what I must share with others (John 15:9).

This community of love is the kingdom of God. The kingdom comprises all those who love God with all their heart, being, strength, and mind, and who love their neighbors as themselves (Luke 10:25–28). The kingdom is not a place, but a state of being (Luke 17:20–21).

Prayer, then, is cooperation with God in restoring God's image within me. God always makes the initial effort, and God sustains whatever effort I can muster. Indeed, without God we cannot pray at all. However, I may either accept or reject the invitation. To accept the invitation is prayer. Important as it is to accept the invitation, such acceptance marks only the first steps in prayer. To advance in prayer, to make the image within me glimmer, I must cooperate more and more with God. That cooperation must grow continuously, growing ever more deep and mature until I am empty of self (Gen 5:24), and only God remains.

CHAPTER EIGHT

Purity

"Blessed are the pure in heart, for they will see God."

Matthew 5:8

Union with God, the restoration of the divine image within us, is the goal of humanity. The springboard to our oneness with God is purity of heart, without which union with God is impossible. Though purity of heart is certainly a virtue, it is not a goal in and of itself. It is merely a means to the ultimate goal: God. The goal of the farmer is not to till the fields for planting, but a bountiful harvest. Similarly, the goal of the Christian is to prepare the heart for restoration of God's image; a pure heart is the means.

Chastity and modesty do not define purity of heart, though they are certainly a component of it. Purity of heart goes far beyond sexual ethics. Purity of heart is freedom from disturbance, a tranquility of the soul, a deep inner peace, a calming of the passions, a wholeness. Purity of heart is the ground bed for prayer. The greater my purity of heart, the deeper will be my prayer.

Purity of heart is undaunted by external influences. Attempts to ground purity of heart in external safeguards is doomed to failure. Flight to remote locations, escape to one's room, shelter in cliques, refuge in piety are all false security. Eventually these external safeguards crumble like a house of cards. This is not to say that we should shun like-minded persons, avoid retreats, or ignore solitude. However, if purity of heart rests upon such things, then one does not possess purity of heart; one possesses crutches, and rickety ones at that. For the battle for purity of heart is an internal struggle (Matt 23:25).

Purity of heart is found in humility. Humility is the realization that I am not the agent for my existence or salvation, but rather that both come from God. The humble Christian knows that the kingdom of God can neither be earned nor imposed by humanity. No piety, no moral effort can buy it. No political system, either civil or ecclesiastical, can implement it. I am totally dependent upon God for the gift of the kingdom. Humility, then, is the total dependence of the person upon God.

Humility strikes at the heart of the "false self." The false self is the self that is developed in my own likeness rather than in the likeness of God. It bases its existence, not upon God, but upon the self. Jesus taught us to deny ourselves, take up our cross, and follow him. The false self teaches us to indulge ourselves, refuse the cross, and follow nobody. The false self is alienation, not just from God, but from my true self, which is the image of God within me.

The false self is the product of fear. It is constructed over the years, constantly adjusted and reformed, in order to thwart danger and to bolster esteem. The false self is what I want you to see and believe about me. It is a projection of attributes the prevailing culture values.

Freedom and the false self cannot coexist, because the false self perpetually demands action to justify its existence. The false self is never satisfied with simply *being*, it requires *doing*, for only in doing can the false self justify its existence. Hence, under the burden of the false self, I am never free to simply *be*. With the false self I can never relax, for I must perpetually justify my existence by doing something.

The ally of the false self is pride. Pride promises honor where there is shame, power where there is impotence. Pride is the tool the false self uses to motivate its perpetuation. Pride reminds me that others are an obstacle to my personal fulfillment, and that they are to be used only for my self-aggrandizement. The false self, then, not only alienates myself from God, it estranges me from my neighbor.

The false self is a lie, an illusion. It settles for the superficial instead of the real. Capitulation to superficiality eventually results in frustration and disillusionment, for by settling for the superficial I become alienated from my true inner self, which is the image of God, and I also become estranged from my neighbor.

If humility consumes the false self, what remains when the false self has been vanquished?

Emptiness.

Completely empty of the false self, I now can see myself as I really am: a child of God in Christ. Free of the burden to create an image of myself, free of the yoke to perpetually justify myself, I now discern that I am known and loved by God. I now can relax, for I have no need to project a false image that will prop up my self-esteem, a self-made image concocted in order to make people love me. I have no need of that, because I am safe and secure in the love of God. As Psalm 27:1 says:

The LORD is my light and my salvation;
    whom shall I fear?
The LORD is the stronghold of my life;
    of whom shall I be afraid?

Now, I can simply *be*. I become…real. Abandoning the false self and discovering the image of God within me is *the* existential moment of my life. I am empty of the stony heart of my own creation, and in its place God has restored my natural heart (Ezek 11:19). That natural heart is the image of God living within me. Feeling secure in the love of God and in his protection, I am now free to love God in the manner expected of me. More importantly, however, I now love God in the manner in which I desire to love God: with all my strength, mind, soul, and body. As St. John Climacus observed, "Love and humility make a holy team."[1]

Furthermore, liberation from the false self waters the seeds of charity. Since I fathom that I am God's image, my eyes also open to the fact that my neighbor is that image as well. I no longer see my neighbor as an object. Thus, the charity God has shown me in Christ, I show in return to my neighbor. But my relations with my neighbor go beyond charity. I must strive to enter spiritually with my neighbor, to see my neighbor as Christ sees him or her, to love my neighbor as *another* self. As St. John Climacus writes, "He who loves the Lord has first loved his brother, for the latter is proof of the former."[2]

Stripping myself of the false self, becoming humble, is neither quick nor easy. It requires a lifetime and constant conversion. I cannot be humble through my own efforts, either. Cooperation with the Holy Spirit is necessary. But all this brings up the question: How is such humility achieved?

CHAPTER NINE

Word

> Strive in every way to devote yourself constantly to the sacred reading so that continuous meditation will seep into your soul and, as it were, will shape it to its image.
>
> *Cassian*, Conferences *(14.10)*

The Bible is the window to God. Through the Bible I learn who God is, how God has intervened in history, and what God wants from me. The Bible is about a relationship, a relationship between Creator and creature, more specifically, between God and the Church. The purpose of the Bible is to portray the covenant between God and creatures.

Prayer is the means to relating to God. The Bible is a book of revelation leading to a response: prayer. It is not a tool to debate this or that theory of science, or this or that model of church. Neither is the Bible a battleground for "proving" one religion "true" and another religion "false." The Bible is not a club with which to bludgeon one's theological opponent with "proofs." The Bible does not "prove" anything; it is neither a scientific treatise nor a logistic syllogism. Rather, the Bible invites us to encounter God in faith.

Reading the Bible is not like reading a novel. Nor is reading the Bible like reading a history book or a how-to-fix-it book. The Bible is not meant to be read from cover to cover. To flop down in your chair, flip open the Bible to Genesis, and try to plow your way through to Revelation is to invite disaster.

The Bible should be digested in small chunks. Read it aloud, but softly. Linger over chapters, chew on verses, read and reflect. Most of all, *listen*. Reading the Bible is not so much about reading the words on the page as it is listening to God after you have read a passage. Nothing coming to you after you have read verse five, then move on to verse six. What word or phrase jumps out at you? Read the word or the phrase again. Gnaw on it, mull it over. Listen. And remember: there is no time limit. So what if eighteen months are required to read through John's Gospel?

Listening teaches humility. Listening implies that the one to whom you are listening has something you do not. Listening differs from hearing. On my drive to work in the mornings, I hear the radio, but I *listen* when the traffic reporter warns of the wreck up the road. To open up the Bible and proclaim, "I'm going to read a chapter a day," is one thing. To open up the Bible and say, "I'm going to listen to God," is another. As Paul Evdokimov notes, "Humility places the axis of a human being in God."[1]Scripture is the vehicle for the spiritual journey. To travel from point A to point B, I can walk, drive, fly, or take a train. The journey of the spirit requires a mode of "transportation" as well. That mode is Scripture. It is the vehicle that transports us with God.

Notice I said "*with* God," instead of "*to* God." If the journey were to God, the implication would be that, at some point along the way in the journey, God was not with me, that I was traveling alone without God, who was "waiting" for me at some point in the distance, either far or near. Such thinking is erroneous. God is always with us. Jesus is Emmanuel: "God is with us" (Matt 1:23). The Acts of the Apostles says that people "would search for God and perhaps grope for him and find him— though indeed he is not far from each one of us" (Acts 17:27). Even when I am seemingly adrift, God is there. In fact, there is no place I can be where God is not.

> Where can I go from your spirit,
>   or where can I flee from your presence?
> If I ascend to heaven, you are there;
>   if I make my bed in Sheol, you are there.

59

If I take the wings of the morning
    and settle at the farthest limits of the sea,
even there your hand shall lead me,
    and your right hand shall hold me fast.
    (Ps 139:7–10)

A physical journey is from point A to point B. The spiritual journey is not. The spiritual journey is about disappearing. Since God is always with us, the closer I allow God to draw me to himself, the more I disappear and the more God appears in me. In other words, the spiritual journey is about disappearing into God.

God makes this "disappearing act" simple for us. In the Book of Amos we read: "Seek me and live" (Amos 5:4) The pericope does not say: "Find me, that you may live." All that is necessary is the seeking. But seek God with a sincere heart. Remember, the principal agent of action in this journey is not us, but God. Our responsibility is to accept the action God stirs within us. God handles the rest.

In the Scriptures, then, we meet Christ. Now, there are two approaches to studying the Bible. One can study it in an academic manner, or one can pray it in a devotional manner. Either way is valid, but for our purposes here the Bible is a prayer book. As a form of prayer, the Christian reads, digests, and meditates upon the Word of God. The point is to allow the text to transform us in Christ. I climb the mountain of Scripture and become transfigured in Christ, just as Jesus climbed the mountain and was transfigured and showed forth the glory of the Father. In both instances, God was and is the agent of action. Therefore, in praying the Scriptures, I must be patient and allow God to transform me in the manner and time God sees fit. My duty is merely to pray, and to pray always. How is that done?

CHAPTER TEN

Always

Pray without ceasing.

1 Thessalonians 5:17

When I first started making retreats at New Melleray Abbey, a Trappist monastery in Iowa, I thought it important to pray during my work assignments. Consequently, while I was picking green beans or washing tomatoes or sanding down caskets, I would pray an Our Father or a Hail Mary or some other prayer. Gradually, though, I came to realize that the beans I was picking or the tomatoes I was washing or the caskets I was sanding could itself be prayer. Work could be prayer.

Paul's admonition to pray always does not mean that I must constantly be rattling off Our Fathers, Hail Marys, the Chaplet of the Divine Mercy, the Litany of the Saints, or the Divine Praises. Nor that I must have a mental picture of Jesus or Mary or the saints perpetually plastered on my brain. Nor that I must always be thinking "holy thoughts." Nor that I must always be fighting off "bad thoughts." Of course, Paul's admonition to pray always does not exclude any of those things, either. Yet, Paul's admonition is commonly interpreted to mean to be always praying *something*, and a portion, if not all, of the above listings is usually invoked.

Paul has something altogether different in mind. First of all, the Hail Mary, the Chaplet of the Divine Mercy, and the Litany of the Saints were composed long after Paul, so he could not even have had anything like that in mind. No, what Paul is talking about when he insists that we pray always is a state of being.

To pray always means to be in a constant state of closeness with God, in constant communion with God. Constant prayer is to rest in God. Words are not even necessary. In fact, the deeper you go in prayer, the fewer words you want to use. As Alexander Schmemann wrote: "As one approaches the essence of a thing, fewer and fewer words are needed."[1] They merely get in the way. Images, too, become a mere hindrance in deep prayer. I am not talking about statues and icons inside churches, but images conjured up in the mind to aid prayer. Even visions of sacred things can be an impediment when all you desire to do is rest in the love of God.

Listen to Nicodemos of the Holy Mountain:

Because God transcends all beings both visible and invisible, the human mind seeking to be united with God through prayer must go out of all beings that are perceptible or intelligible in order to achieve this divine union.[2]

Resting in God is the goal of perpetual prayer. You cannot rest if you are constantly doing something, even if that something is praying. "'Be still, and know that I am God'" (Ps 46:10), we are instructed. Don't become enslaved to compulsive routines, no matter how pious they be. Be it the Divine Office, the Rosary, novenas, or whatever, don't be compulsive about it. Habitual, yes, but not compulsive. The difference? When a routine is habitual, you are in control of the habit; compulsive, and the compulsion is in charge of you.

The purpose for resting in God is twofold. First, resting in God brings you peace. Second, resting in God allows God to work in you. Remember, God is the principal agent of action in prayer, not you. God changes you through prayer. God does so by working the fallow field of your spirit. If your spirit is "filled with beans," how is God going to plant the corn?

Prayer is neither technique nor style, but being receptive to God. You have to remain open to God in order to allow God to work in you. This openness to God, this constantly being receptive to God, is the essence of unceasing prayer.

Openness to God, however, can become blocked by distractions. Distractions are any thought, image, or sensation that inhibits you from resting in God. Distractions are not necessarily "bad thoughts." Distractions can also be good or holy thoughts, images, or sensations. They are distractions because, when you dwell on such thoughts, you are dwelling on the attributes of God, and not God himself. So the first thing to understand about distractions is that they are not necessarily "bad"; they just get in the way.

The second thing to understand about thoughts or distractions is that no matter how "bad" they may be, such thoughts do not make you a "bad" person. Acting out such thoughts is another matter, but the random, fleeting thoughts that race or float through our minds are not to be taken seriously. They are a part of the fallen human condition.

So the real question about distractions is not their intrinsic worth (whether or not they are good or bad). The real question is how to handle them.

A colossal mistake in dealing with distractions is to try to suppress thoughts, to make the mind go blank. Impossible. Cannot be achieved. God gave you a brain, and your brain is always "on." You cannot click it off. Therefore, the manner in which to handle distractions must lie elsewhere.

The answer is that you redirect your thoughts. During prayer, when distractions attack, acknowledge them and simply allow them to pass by.

When I was a child we used to picnic sometimes on the banks of the Ohio River. down in Harrison or Crawford County. I recall sitting in the grass watching the river float by. Now and then a barge would chug along. Soon, though, it would be out of sight, and once again all I would see was the river itself.

In prayer, distractions are the barge, while the river itself—God—is the focal point. We didn't picnic on the banks of the Ohio River to view barges; if we wanted to see barges, we could have driven over to Jeff Boat in Jeffersonville to watch them being built. The attraction was the river itself. In prayer, your intention is to rest in God, to relax in watching the river float by. Distractions are anything that hinders that intention.

Notice I said your *intention* is to rest in God. In prayer, we do not pay attention to God. To "pay attention" while in prayer is to assume that we are concentrating on an entity not with us, not a part of us, but who is someplace else. The whole purpose of prayer, however, is to rest in God. Enoch is a prime example of this. "Enoch walked with God; then he was no more, because God took him" (Gen 5:24). In prayer, our intention is to be completely enveloped by God so that we disappear and all that remains is God.

One way to handle distractions that hinder such envelopment is to revert to a sacred word. When you are in prayer, and you begin to pay attention to distractions, return to a sacred word of your choosing. The word can be any word: Jesus, Father, Spirit, peace, love, maranatha, and so on. Slowly and gently and quietly repeat the sacred word until the distractions run their course, then gently and softly allow the sacred word to drift away from you, until you are once more quiet. The purpose of the word is to draw your attention from the distractions. The sacred word, in and of itself, has no other meaning than to verbalize your intention of return to resting in God. By invoking the sacred word, you are demonstrating that you will not be dominated by your thoughts, but that you intend to be enveloped by God. This form of prayer has a name: Centering Prayer.

In Centering Prayer you delve within yourself, only to finally transcend yourself and rest in God. One frequent, but unfounded, criticism of Centering Prayer is that it is "worshiping oneself." Nothing could be further from the truth. In Centering Prayer you delve within yourself, because you meet God in the very "core" of your being (Luke 17:21). Yet, you do not remain within yourself, but are transformed by God beyond yourself. As the author of *The Cloud of Unknowing* writes:

> There will come times when your mind is free of involvement with anything material or spiritual and totally taken up with the being of God himself....At such times you transcend yourself, becoming almost divine, though you remain beneath God. I say you

have transcended yourself, because you have gained by grace what is impossible to you by nature, for this union with God is the gift of grace.[3]

In prayer God draws us to himself by first coming to us. Prayer is nothing more than the incarnation made personal. Just as God drew us to himself by coming to us in the person of Jesus of Nazareth, so in prayer God draws us to himself, not by waiting for us to come to him, but by first coming to us. Then, God draws us out of ourselves by completely over-shadowing us. The goal is to completely disappear in God, not in ourselves. The irony, of course, is that all this begins with delving to the center of ourselves. As Nicodemos of the Holy Mountain wrote, "Everybody finds calm and rest at their center."[4]

Centering Prayer, then, seeks not to avoid distractions, but to successfully deal with them. But if my Centering Prayer is to be successful, I must place this prayer in a context conducive to prayer. I cannot practice Centering Prayer, or any other kind of prayer, in the inappropriate environment.

What is the inappropriate environment? What is the appropriate one?

CHAPTER ELEVEN

Silence

Be still, and know that I am God.

Psalm 46:10

Silence is the mother of prayer.[1]

St. John Climacus

Have you attended a Major League Baseball game lately? How about a NBA game? NHL? If you have, you probably noticed that between innings or timeouts or periods there is a lot of noise. I am not talking about the fans. I'm talking about the loud music piped over the PA, the funny games or stunts out on the court or field, and the dancing pom-pom girls. The last time I attended a White Sox game, the time between innings was filled with either loud music or stunts. The impression I received from all this was that management was terrified that, if the park grew quiet between innings, the people in the stands, deprived of entertainment even for brief moments, would bolt.

Remember the last time you drove your car? Chances are, you had the radio turned on or the CD player. If not listening to music or news, perhaps you were listening to a lecture or a novel. Doing this fills the time. Such behavior is not limited to driving long distances either. The drive to the convenience store requires mere minutes, but you have it cranked up. I know because I do it myself.

I am not suggesting that sports arenas should be hushed houses of prayer. Nor am I implying that people at such venues should be restrained from raising a little hell (the key word is "little"). Furthermore, I am not advocating ripping out radios and CD players from automobiles. I am suggesting, however, that for the most part, we modern Americans are afraid of being quiet.

Silence is both the medium and milieu of prayer. It is at the same time the language in which prayer is spoken and the environment in which it is practiced. This is not to say, of course, that one cannot pray amid noise. A Muslim acquaintance of mine tells of praying one of his five daily prayers near a ride at Disney World in Orlando.

For the most part, however, prayer is prayed in silence. Jesus is the perfect model for going off and praying alone amid the quiet. Jesus "went out to the mountain to pray; and he spent the night in prayer to God" (Luke 6:12).

More and more people are seeking deserted places in which to pray, reflect, and delve into silence.

Often these places are monasteries. There one retreats from the cacophony of daily life. Some monasteries have no radio, televisions, or CD players to distract you. Instead, the monastery has a room with a bed, a desk, a Bible, and a cross on the wall. You enter this room. You pray.

While in that room, you go on a journey, for prayer is a journey. The journey might be resplendent with ecstasies, or the journey may be fraught with fear, ennui, or angst. In either case, you take nothing with you on this journey. Oh, you may have brought a book or a diary or a rosary to the monastery with you. Yet, on the journey itself, you take nothing. Jesus said to his disciples, "Take no gold or silver, or copper in your belts, no bag for your journey, or two tunics, or sandals, or a staff" (Matt 10:9–10). On your journey to God, God wants only *you*. The journey with God, prayer, is about letting go of things, any *thing* that hinders your union with God. When you have let go, you become empty. By your becoming empty, God is able to fill you up with himself so that you become filled with grace: the shining image of God. As is written in 1 Peter 2:10: "Once you were not a people, but now you are God's people." We become God's people by first becoming open to God's purposes. Jim Forest writes, "God is not an idea and praying is not an exercise to improve our idea of God....Prayer is the cultivation of the awareness of God's actual presence."[2]

Cultivating an awareness of God's presence means becoming attentive. Becoming aware of God means abandoning even the consolations of prayer. Becoming open is the prayer itself. Therefore, to pray is to empty oneself to the point of nothingness. This is no abstract philosophical concept. Rather, it is the foundational basis of prayer and something Our Lord Jesus practiced. St. Paul writes that Jesus "emptied himself, taking the form of a slave" (Phil 2:7). To empty oneself, then, is precisely to follow the Master. Yet, this emptying to nothingness is not the goal in and of itself. Emptying has only one purpose: to be filled up with God, to become the slave of God, just as Jesus did. Emptying oneself requires silence and solitude, hence Jesus' frequent flights to deserted places to pray.

Emptying oneself also requires effort. Silence and solitude are key, but you must insert that key into the lock and turn it before the lock can be unlatched. Make time, then, for silence. Find a place to be alone. St. John Climacus wrote that a person desiring to pray, but who is distracted, is "like a man who expects to walk quickly even though his legs are tied together."[3] Early morning hours, before everyone else is up, may be the time for your silence and solitude. Not a morning person? Turn off Letterman or Leno and make late night your retreat.

Silence and solitude quiet the soul, make it still, allowing the soul to empty itself of distractions that separate it from God. The quiet soul—stillness—is one receptive to God. He or she who has achieved stillness is on the threshold of contemplation.

CHAPTER TWELVE

Contemplation

Contemplation is listening in silence, an expectancy.[1]

Thomas Merton

Contemplation is not sitting around "gazing at your navel." Contemplation is not sitting in the lotus position amid billowing clouds of incense, chanting "ommm." Contemplation is not something only monks do. Contemplation is not the antithesis of action in the world.

Contemplation is the Christian life grounded in loving attention. The only purpose of prayer is to share in the life of Christ. The contemplative listens for the question God asked in Genesis when the Lord God moved about in the garden at the breezy time of day: "Where are you?" The Christian's reply echoes Samuel's: "Speak, for your servant is listening" (1 Sam 3:10).

Merton is correct in saying that contemplation is listening. It is sustained listening. More than anything, contemplation is an attitude, a way of life. The contemplative arranges his or her whole life so that he or she can listen more carefully to God. Anybody can do this at anytime. The practice of arranging one's life in order to listen to God is called prayer.

In a classroom you listen to the instructor by paying attention. At work you listen to your supervisor by paying attention. At home you listen to and watch a television program by paying attention. Just the opposite is true in prayer. In prayer you listen by *not* paying attention. In prayer you listen by letting go. In fact, in prayer you listen by not listening at all, for you are not trying to "hear" anything. In prayer you are not anticipating any kind of message or sign, either verbal or visual. To anticipate anything while in prayer is not to be praying in the first place, but to be bartering: "I will sit here quietly thinking about you, if you do this for me." Bartering is not prayer. Evagrius is blunt about this: "Do not by any means strive to fashion some image or visualize some form at the time of prayer."[2]

Contemplative prayer is surrendering the self to God. Jesus surrendered himself to the Father even to the point of death. The Gospel of John says that Jesus "gave up his spirit" (John 19:30). Now, few Christians are called to surrender to the point of physical death, that is, to be martyrs. But all Christians must take up their cross and follow Christ.

Surrendering to God is nothing other than resting in the love of God. God cannot be grasped, for God is not an object. We cannot "know" God totally. We can know *of* him, but our finite brains cannot comprehend the infinite. We can, however, love God. The anonymous author of *The Cloud of Unknowing* put it this way:

> No one can fully comprehend the uncreated God with his knowledge, but each one, in a different way, can grasp him fully through love…for man was created to love and everything else was created to make love possible.[3]

Prayer, then, is surrendering to the love God has for us. Prayer is reflecting back to God that love he first gives to us. The brighter God's image shines in us, the brighter will be the love we reflect back to him.

But contemplation is not merely a "me and God" relationship. The Christian is called to a community, the Church, and we show our love for God by loving our neighbor. Yes, Jesus "would withdraw to deserted places and pray" (Luke 5:16), but when Jesus began his ministry he also said the Lord had anointed him to "bring good news to the poor. He has sent me to proclaim release to the captives and recovery of sight to the blind, to let the oppressed go free, and to proclaim the year of the Lord's favor" (Luke 4:18–19).

The contemplative, the person of prayer, does not compartmentalize his or her life. It is completely foreign to the contemplative to have a "prayer life" and "a regular life." Prayer, to the contemplative, is not something that is tacked on. No, for the contemplative, prayer *is* life. Life is meaningless and void without prayer. As Merton said:

> There is no meaning to life, except in man seeking God and God seeking man. Man's life has no natural meaning apart from the supernatural, and man's nature has no meaning except in so far as it is ordered to supernatural fulfillment....[Life] has no meaning unless it refers to this business of me seeking God and God seeking me.[4]

The laity has much to gain by embracing the contemplative life, for contemplation reveals Jesus in the world of everyday life, and thus reveals Jesus in the stranger, in the oppressed, in the hungry, and in the forgotten. Recall Jesus' words before gathering for the last time with his disciples at the Last Supper: "For I was hungry and you gave me food, I was thirsty and you gave me something to drink, I was a stranger and you welcomed me, I was naked and you gave me clothing, I was sick and you took care of me, I was in prison and you visited me" (Matt 25:35–36). In that way, contemplation and justice go hand in hand. However, contemplation without justice is narcissism, while justice without contemplation can be mere legalism.

Contemplation and justice are opposite sides of the same coin called love. Love, the prophet Hosea tells us, is what God desires: "For I desire steadfast love and not sacrifice" (Hos 6:6). St. Paul wrote that in the end, when all is said and done, only three things last: faith, hope, and love, and that the greatest of those three things is love. More than faith. More than hope. Why is love such a premium? Because "God is love" (1 John 4:8). Since we are created in God's image, which essentially is love, then we are created in order to love. To love is to treat our brothers and sisters with justice. Justice requires reflection, which is contemplation. Contemplation is resting in God, a God of love.

CHAPTER THIRTEEN

Holy

For I am the LORD your God; sanctify yourselves
therefore and be holy, for I am holy.

Leviticus 11:44

T he goal is to be holy, not to be good. Anyone
can be good. The pagan, the atheist, and the
agnostic can live ethical lives and be out-
standing pillars of the community.

Christians, on the other hand, are called not
merely to be good but to be holy. St. Peter echoes
Leviticus when he writes in his epistle, "As he who
called you is holy, be holy yourselves" (1 Pet 1:15).
Because we are created in God's image, and because
God is holy, we must be holy as well. Otherwise, we
cannot reflect the image of God; otherwise we reflect,
not God, but ourselves.

We cannot manufacture holiness. We cannot be holy on our own accord. Only God is holy, and only God can grant us holiness.

Holiness is intimately linked to the mysteries of redemption: incarnation, resurrection, and pentecost. Through the incarnation, God became one of us. Paul Evdokimov rightly says, "This participation of God in the human is decisive."[1] It is decisive, because without God entering into human history as Jesus of Nazareth, humanity would lack the revelation disclosing God's life. Raymond E. Brown articulated this idea well:

> Unless we understand that Jesus was truly human with no exception but sin, we cannot comprehend the depth of God's love....A Jesus who walked through the world with unlimited knowledge, knowing exactly what the morrow would bring, knowing with certainty that three days after his death his Father would raise him up, would be a Jesus who could arouse our admiration, but a Jesus still far from us. He would be a Jesus far from a humankind that can only hope in the future and believe in God's goodness, far from a humankind that must face the supreme uncertainty of death with faith but without knowledge of what is beyond. On the other hand, a Jesus for whom the detailed future had elements of mystery,

dread, and hope as it has for us and yet, at the same time, a Jesus who could say, "Not my will but yours"—this would be a Jesus who could effectively teach us how to live, for this Jesus would have gone through life's real trials. Then his saying, "No one can have greater love than this: to lay down his life for those he loves" (John 15:13), would be truly persuasive, for we would know that he laid down his life with all the agony with which we lay ours down. We would know that for him the loss of life was, as it is for us, the loss of a great possession, a possession that is outranked only by love.[2]

Through the cross and resurrection, God redeemed us. St. Paul boils the faith down to a nutshell when he said: "If Christ has not been raised, your faith is futile and you are still in your sins" (1 Cor 15:17). The resurrection completes what the incarnation began.

But pentecost crowns creation by giving us God's Spirit. This is not to say that pentecost makes us God. Rather, pentecost makes us like God in that we are consumed with God's Spirit. The Second Letter of Peter goes so far as to say that we humans "become participants of the divine nature" (2 Pet 1:4). We undergo divinization, as is said in the Eastern Church. It is pentecost that enables us to live the incarnation and hope in the resurrection. Pentecost allows us to love unconditionally.

Holiness, then, is at its core trinitarian. Holiness is the Spirit of God the Father working in us through the Risen Christ. Holiness is a process by which God brings us back to himself by slowly revealing himself to us. This revelation began with Adam and culminates in Christ and the Spirit. Our task is to be open and discerning to that revelation.

For the universal call to holiness is truly that: universal. The Second Vatican Council made clear that the call to holiness is not just limited to the clergy, nor is it limited to the laity within the Church. The universal call to holiness is issued to all humanity. The Lord Jesus "sent the Holy Spirit upon all…that He might inspire them from within to love God" (*Lumen Gentium* 40). Also this: "Holiness is cultivated by all who are moved by the Spirit of God, and who obey the voice of the Father, worshipping God the Father in spirit and in truth" (*Lumen Gentium* 41). The Jew, the Christian, the Muslim, and others whom God has touched, are all called to be holy. Furthermore, because holiness is open to all, it is expected of all. Holiness is not just for the "professional" pray-ers: clergy, monks, and nuns. Holiness is for everyone.

This holiness, which is everyone's vocation, in essence re-creates humanity. Of course, humanity always has the freedom to refuse this call to holiness, and it does so daily. Such refusal is deemed sin. Paul Evdokimov said of such freedom, "The titanic power of rejecting God is the ultimate human freedom."[3] But such abuse of freedom does not deter God from continuing to call us to lives of love. Indeed, God searches even more diligently for us precisely because of our sin. Jesus illustrated this diligence of God in the parable of the prodigal son (Luke 15:1–31).

Holiness is being filled with the Holy Spirit, and the Holy Spirit knows no boundaries, whether ecclesiastical, political, clerical, or lay. A person filled with the Holy Spirit has a burning desire for God, which is one of the reasons why our image for the Holy Spirit is often fire. The person transformed by the Spirit is on fire with God's love and mercy. God's call to holiness sparks prayer. Prayer illuminates God's image for all to see. The irony is that, as you delve deeper and deeper into prayer, and as you assume more and more the likeness of God, the less other people are actually seeing you; what they are actually seeing is God. For holiness, salvation, is like Enoch at Genesis 5:24: "Enoch walked with God; then he was no more, because God took him." Salvation is about holiness, which is about disappearing into the image of God.

CHAPTER FOURTEEN

Transformation

Having seen how prayer is participation with God in God's work to transform us—that is, to save us—we now return to the idea that salvation today should be seen as a transformative process rather than a juridical event.

This dialectic between the transformative and the juridical is nothing new. It goes all the way back to Paul and John. For Paul, the beginning and end of faith is "Jesus Christ, and him crucified" (1 Cor 2:2). Jesus' death "redeemed us from the curse of the law" (Gal 3:13). Humanity, because of its sin, was under the curse of the law, but God made Jesus "to be sin...so that in him we might become the righteousness of God (2 Cor 5:21). Humanity becomes righteous in the eyes of God, because Jesus' death is "a sacrifice...by his blood" (Rom 3:25). In other words, Jesus, the sinless one, takes our place in death, a death that humanity deserves. Thus, humanity is reconciled with God or, as Paul puts it, "reconciled...through the cross" (Eph 2:16).

Jesus' death, however, is not the end. Just as important as the death of Jesus is his resurrection: "If Christ has not been raised, your faith is futile and you are still in your sins....Just as all die in Adam, so all will be made alive in Christ" (1 Cor 15:17, 22). So for Paul the crucifixion and the resurrection comprise a single event, albeit in two parts. What is of utmost importance for Paul, however, is that this single event in two parts reconciles humanity to God. Jesus' death and resurrection redeems humanity. In modern parlance, it is through this event that "we are saved."

Paul's theology is rooted in his road-to-Damascus experience. Paul never knew Jesus of Nazareth, but on the road to Damascus he was spectacularly introduced to the Risen Christ. Whereas it is absolutely true that the Risen Christ and Jesus of Nazareth are one in the same, it is nonetheless true that Paul experienced only the risen Christ. Consequently, Paul's theology is colored by those events that produce this Risen Christ: the death and resurrection. For Paul, this is what is real to him. This is not to say that Paul is unaware of Jesus' birth, life, and ministry. Rather, the experience of the Risen Christ is so powerful for Paul that it subdues all other aspects of Jesus Christ.

John approaches Jesus from a different angle. For John, the beginning and end of faith is that "the

Word became flesh and lived among us" (John 1:14). Jesus is God, comes from God, and is among us. Though no one has ever seen God (John 1:18), Jesus of Nazareth is so filled with God that Jesus can truthfully say, "Whoever has seen me has seen the Father" (John 14:9). At the same time, Jesus differentiates between himself and the Father by saying, "The Father is greater than I" (John 14:28). However, the very purpose for Jesus to have assumed flesh and lived among us is for us humans to "realize that I [Jesus] am in my Father, and you in me, and I in you" (John 14:20). When we realize that—when we come to *believe* that—we are saved: "For God so loved the world that he gave his only Son, so that everyone who believes in him may not perish but may have eternal life" (John 3:16). We are saved because by believing and understanding that God is in us and we are in God, we begin the process of transformation that takes us from death to life. For that which is of God can never truly die.

This belief—that Jesus is in the Father, and that we are in Jesus, and that Jesus is in us—is confirmed by the death and resurrection of Jesus. If the Father had not been in Jesus, Jesus would never have resurrected. For Paul, the death and resurrection of Jesus is the juridical process that makes us right with God. For John, the death and resurrection of Jesus is the verification that the Father is in Jesus. Since we too are in Jesus, and he in us, then we "rise" with Jesus as well.

If Paul's theology is rooted in the road-to-Damascus experience, John's theology is rooted in the washing of the disciples' feet (John 13:1–20). Just as Jesus stoops down to wash the disciples' feet, so God stoops to humanity to cleanse it. To cleanse humanity, God must touch us, just as Jesus touches the disciples' feet. This touching is the divine and human coming together.

But it does not end there. Toward the conclusion of the feet-washing episode, Jesus tells his disciples that just as he has washed their feet, so they must wash one another's (John 13:14). Similarly, just as God touches us and brings us into him, and he into us, so we must go forth and touch our neighbor, so that God can bring them to himself though us.

In other words, the whole process of salvation for John is not a juridical action on the part of God that makes humanity right with God, but a process of transformation into the likeness of God, what the Eastern Church calls divinization. That is what makes humanity right with God.

To oversimplify in order to highlight the difference between Paul and John: Paul is interested in what Jesus *does*; John is interested in who Jesus *is*. Neither approach, however, is "correct" and the other "incorrect." Both approaches stem from Scripture and are handed down in the Tradition; both are "correct."

It is the contention here, though, that the modern Westerner is in need of knowing *who* Jesus is, not in *what* Jesus does. If the Church can do a better job of conveying *who* Jesus is, the Church will have a better chance—at least in this given moment in history—of conveying what Jesus does: save. But the emphasis must be on the *is*, not the *does*; on the *who*, not the *what*. Thus, for purposes of evangelization, the Church today needs to stress Jesus the person, who invites us to transformation into the image of God.

CHAPTER FIFTEEN

Desire

The formation of a man is...the love of God. For the Love of God, or the Love that is God, the Holy Spirit, attracts him to itself; then God loves himself in man and makes him, his spirit and his love, one with himself.

William of St. Thierry, The Golden Epistle,
no. 169–70

For the twelfth-century Cistercians, salvation was found in loving God. Salvation was becoming one with God; becoming like God. This theme is found over and over again in the writings of William of St. Thierry (ca. 1085–1148) and his friend Bernard of Clairvaux (1090–1148).

What is ironic about this love for God, is that the desire does not stem from the person, but from God. "You should understand," writes Bernard, "that if your soul seeks God, God has sought it....

The desire is the product of God's activity. By itself, the soul is impotent. 'I have the desire to do what is good, but I cannot carry it out' (Rom 7:19)."[1]

Furthermore, this love and desire for God is itself knowledge of God. "For love of God itself is knowledge of him; unless he is loved, he is not known, and unless he is known, he is not loved. He is known only insofar as he is loved, and he is loved only insofar as he is known."[2]

The contention here is that salvation seen in this light is appealing to modern Westerners. So let us take a closer look at the twelfth-century Cistercians, especially Bernard and William.

We begin with Bernard. The abbot of Clairvaux said that the core dignity of humanity resided in the fact that humanity was created in the image and likeness of God (Gen 1:26). What is crucial to Bernard's thought, here, is that despite the fall, humanity never relinquishes the image. The image of God is always imprinted in the very being of the person. Of what does this image consist? For Bernard, the image of God rests in free will. That free will—that image of God imprinted into humanity—is always present. It can never leave humanity.

However, humanity's free will is wounded due to sin. Because of sin, people are marred in directing their free will toward the good; they find it difficult to do so. This ability to direct the will toward the good is, Bernard says, the likeness of God. Thus, what humanity must do is restore the likeness of God so that the image—the free will—can then be directed toward the good. How does humanity do that?

It can't.

God alone can restore the likeness of God. Humanity can only cooperate with God in restoring the likeness.

God is always drawing us to himself in order to help humanity restore the likeness, and God draws us to himself through Jesus the Christ, the image of God. The means by which God draws us to himself through Jesus is love: "For God so loved the world that he gave his only Son" (John 3:16).

Salvation, then, is restoring that which is natural to humanity in the first place: the likeness of God. David Bell puts it well: Salvation is "the process of realizing and actualizing the true nature of something which has been there all the time."[3]

William of St. Thierry had the same idea as Bernard, but with a little twist. William believed that the image of God rested not in free will (as did Bernard), but in love. Humanity, then, has an innate desire for God, and this innate desire for God is *image*. The likeness of God, for William, is the potential for loving. However, that potential has been wounded by sin. Thus, humanity must restore the likeness of God. As with Bernard, however, humanity is unable to do this due to sin. Humanity, then, must rely on the gift of Jesus the Christ, who sacrificed his life for us in order that the likeness be restored. As William writes, "Resemblance to God is the whole of man's perfection....For to this end alone were we created and do we live, to be like God."[4] Furthermore, William says that humanity achieves perfect likeness to God (unity of spirit) when humanity is able to will only what God wills; in other words, when there is no distinction between the will of God and the will of the person. This willing only what God wills is fueled by *love*. "No longer does it merely desire what God desires, not only does it love him, but it is perfect love, so that it can will only what God wills."[5] Humanity desires to will only what God wills precisely because of love. There is no sense of duty or obligation in willing only what God wills. William uses a nice analogy to point this out: "A man believes without any doubt that he is the son of his father and mother. The authority of his father and mother, whom he believes, is so innate in him that he has no desire to refute it, because he loves them."[6]

However, humanity becoming like God means just that: becoming *like* God. Humanity's becoming like God is derived from God, not something innate within humanity. Humanity becomes like God due to God, not due to humanity's own essence or doing. The creature never becomes the Creator. Both Bernard and William would agree with Augustine who wrote, "But [man] was not made in any sense equal, being created by him, not born of him; so to make this point he is image in such a way as to be 'to the image'; that is, he is not equated in perfect parity with God, but approaches him in similarity."[7] Humanity can be like what God is, but humanity can never be God.

For the twelfth-century Cistercians, then, salvation is a process; a process of becoming like God. It is precisely this idea of salvation that would appeal to twenty-first-century Westerners.

I believe this idea of salvation appeals to the modern Westerner for three reasons. First, this view of salvation takes a positive approach as opposed to a negative approach. Salvation is not steeped in what one is not supposed to do. In this approach there is no: "Don't do this. Don't do that." Rather, the approach is through love; love of God, not self. Through this love, one subsequently avoids those things one "should not do," because no one desires to hurt the one he or she loves.

Second, this view of salvation appeals to the dignity of the person. Too often salvation has been so framed that the person is deemed worthless, dirty, or hopeless. The twelfth-century Cistercians understood that though humanity is steeped in sin, humanity always retains the image of God in which he or she was created. Humanity is worth saving.

Third, this view of salvation respects human freedom, the most important virtue prized by modern Westerners. One must choose to love God. If one chooses to love and serve God, it is done so by the free choice of the person.

Just as important, the Church benefits from this view of salvation, too. The Church benefits because this view of salvation comes from the heart of its Tradition. Yet, because this particular view of salvation has not really been emphasized of late, emphasizing it will make the Church appear novel and contemporary. How ironic! That which is old is new again.

CHAPTER SIXTEEN

Church

The fact is that becoming a disciple of Jesus is an essential element of his message. So regardless of how we go on to fill out its shape historically at a later time, the "church" is essentially discipleship of Jesus: following in the footsteps of Jesus to turn many people into a community which bears witness both to the kingdom of God and to Jesus' own career.[1]

Edward Schillebeeckx

The Holy Roman Church must make disciples of Jesus, for that is the reason for her existence. God calls the individual to himself by drawing him or her to the Church, and it is then the Church that provides the means for the person to become like God. How does the Church do that?

By Word and Sacrament. Becoming like God is a process, a process that takes a lifetime. A story has to be absorbed (Word), and that story has to be nourished (Sacrament). Both are needed in order for the person to become like God.

But both have to be wanted by the person, otherwise Church is nothing more than duty, obligation, and code. And that's exactly what God wants of humanity: God wants us to love him. Thus, the fundamental role of the Church is instilling in her flock the love of God, which results in a desire for God, which results in a need for God, which leads to becoming like God. Orthodoxy subsequently follows, natural as rain.

I have a reoccurring nightmare. I walk into the Elsby Building in my hometown of New Albany, Indiana, and I approach an elevator. The elevator doors open, and I either fall down the elevator shaft, or I get onto the elevator, but when the doors open, I can't exit because the doors open up to a wall.

Many times in my thirty-two years of marriage I have been comforted by my wife in the middle of the night after having awoken from this or other nightmares. Over the years I have become accustomed to yearning for her hugs and reassurance whenever I have nightmares. The reverse is also true. She also has reoccurring dreams, and when she has one, I likewise hold her.

"My soul yearns for you in the night," says Isaiah 26:9. Just as I yearn for the embrace of my wife, so we should yearn for God. It is the yearning for God that the Church must instill in people. When my wife comforts me in the middle of the night due to a nightmare, or I hold her, it is not out of a sense of duty or obligation that we do so. It is because we love one another. In other words, doing so is not a burden, it is not a yoke. "For my yoke is easy, and my burden is light," says Jesus (Matt 11:30).

That is the point: love makes the yoke easy, the burden light. God is not about obligation, duty, code, or catechism. God is, as Schillebeeckx says at the heading of this chapter, about a community of disciples gathered around Jesus. Code and catechism are the circumference that encircles the core. The core is loving God and neighbor; the circumference gives shape to the core.

Word and Sacrament are meant to strengthen the core, not the circumference. The Word is Jesus himself, truly present in the community. Eucharist is Jesus himself, truly present in the community. Both are given freely by God to the community; likewise the community gives back to God in love by becoming like God.

The Holy Spirit enables the community to do this. On its own the community—the Church—would be unable to do so. When the apostles with Mary and other holy women were huddled in the upper room, it was the Holy Spirit that overshadowed them all, and it was the Holy Spirit that emboldened them to leave the upper room and go out into the world and tell the good news.

Likewise, it is the Holy Spirit that will enable the Church to focus on instilling in people a love for God, a desire for God. In his 2008 trip to Australia for World Youth Day, Pope Benedict XVI said that the pursuit of the true, the good, and the beautiful is the end for which we make our decisions. He is absolutely correct. I would further suggest that the pursuit of the true, the good, and the beautiful cannot be freely chosen unless the motivation behind the choice is the desire to be like God. Pope Benedict also noted that freedom finds meaning in truth. Again, the Holy Father is absolutely correct. And it is love that seeks the truth which ends in freedom.

That desire, that love, must be the focus of the Church in the decades to come.

CHAPTER SEVENTEEN

Thirst

It is becoming more and more difficult, in our Western societies, to speak in a meaningful way of "salvation." Yet salvation—deliverance from the reality of evil, and the gift of new life and freedom in Christ—is at the heart of the Gospel. We need to discover new and engaging ways of proclaiming this message and awakening a thirst for the fulfillment which only Christ can bring.

Pope Benedict XVI, to the USCCB at the Basilica of the National Shrine of the Immaculate Conception, April 16, 2008

That is exactly what this book has tried to show: that in the modern Western world, evangelization must be born again. Furthermore, the rebirth of evangelization *must* take seriously the whole issue of freedom, which the West so highly (and rightfully) prizes.

What is being proposed here is not something new, nor something beyond the pale of the magisterium. Rather, what is being proposed here is that the Church look back to its own tradition in order to find what it needs to evangelize now.

That tradition of the Church that, I believe, will be most meaningful to the people of today is the tradition of the twelfth-century Cistercians. Bernard of Clairvaux and William of St. Thierry, among others, emphasized the whole idea of the restoration of the likeness of God, divinization. In other words, salvation was wrapped up in human beings—through the grace of God—becoming more and more like God. It is the contention here that salvation viewed in light of the twelfth-century Cistercians is more palpable to the tastes of modern Westerners than is the current view of salvation that stresses the juridical model.

Pope Benedict aptly uses the phrase "awakening a thirst." How do we awake in people today a thirst for God? Unless people are thirsty for God, they will not seek to quench their thirst. The days of the prevailing society or culture exerting pressure upon an individual to seek God, or to attend church, are gone. "Christendom" is dead. It cannot be relied upon as a help in this matter. Our era is the first era since Constantine in which the Church has to rely on itself—rather than on the state or the prevailing culture—in order to help spread the Gospel of Jesus the Christ. The Church is once again on its own. The Church alone now has to instill in the people a thirst for God.

And the people know that. They know that stigma and convention, once powerful tools, are dead. So the people ask: "You say I need Christianity? Show me why. I need salvation? Yeah, says who? I should go to church? Forget it, I'm sleeping in. I should follow your God? Sorry, I'll follow mine."

However, if the Church can instill in people a desire for God, then people will freely choose God. Desire and freedom go together. Evangelization in today's world will succeed only by appealing to the one thing today's world prizes the most: freedom.

The tradition of the twelfth-century Cistercians, I believe, is best suited for bringing about this desire for God. People want to hear that there is something about them that is worthwhile; something that is redeemable; something that is everlasting. The most difficult part of my ministry to inmates at the Indiana State Prison is convincing the men to whom I minister that God loves them and that they are worth being redeemed by God.

Thus, salvation is not about living up to code or creed, but about becoming more and more like God. William of St. Thierry is emphatic about this: "Faith, Hope and Charity...the Holy Trinity has constituted this trinity to His image and likeness. By it we are renewed in the inner person to the image of him who created us. This is the fabric of human salvation."[1] Subsequently, the more we are configured into the likeness of God, the more we live up to code and creed.

In other words, this schema of salvation respects the dignity of the human person, a dignity the modern Westerner demands. This dignity is freedom. Salvation, then, is nothing other than the proper alignment of freedom, which in turn allows for a proper relationship between humanity and God, and a proper relationship among human beings. As Luke Timothy Johnson notes:

> Sin is not a matter of the spirit being polluted by the body, nor is it a matter of people being enslaved by an unjust social order. It is a disease of freedom itself that is so profound, so complex, so entrenched, so enslaved, that only God has power enough of knowledge and love to redirect that freedom rightly. Salvation is not about getting right knowledge of the self, nor about creating the right political order; it is about being in right relationship with God. And only God can make that relationship right.[2]

The place where that right relationship with God is fostered, nurtured, and fed is in the Church. The Church fosters, nurtures, and feeds this right relationship, I believe, by encouraging *lectio*, tradition, and meditation, or put another way: Scripture, Christian classics, and prayer.

Lectio. The Church must once again encourage the *praying* of Scripture. Bible studies are welcome and important; knowledge of the way the Bible was put together, by whom, and when is necessary. *Lectio*, however, is vital. Being nourished by Scripture is just as important as being nourished by the Body and Blood of Christ. As Jerome said, "Ignorance of Scripture is ignorance of Christ." Scripture makes us hungry for the Body and Blood of the Lord, and vice versa. Scripture and Eucharist work in tandem.

Furthermore, *lectio* requires silence, and silence fosters listening. Remember, in lectio we listen to God.

Tradition. In this book I have extolled the value of the beliefs and writings of the twelfth-century Cistercians. However, the Church has two thousand years of wise men and women who ground modern Christians in the tradition of our faith. We need to mine the wisdom in their writings. They force us moderns to realize that the Church does not simply revolve around us, but that the Church includes all of those who came before us as well, and that they have something valuable to say to us.

Meditation. Reading Christian classics and being nourished by Scripture in *lectio* leads to meditation, which is nothing other than resting in God. This resting in God is the goal of the Christian life.

Thus, these three—*lectio*, Christian classics, and meditation—help bring about that which the Church has always striven to bring about: conversion and self-surrender. Conversion from sin to life; surrender from self to God. Then...*then* we are like Enoch who "walked with God; then he was no more, because God took him" (Gen 5:24); and as we disappear into the image of God we are finally, and forever, free.

CHAPTER EIGHTEEN

Oremus

"O God, you are my God, I seek you, my soul thirsts for you; my flesh faints for you, as in a dry and weary land where there is no water," says the psalmist (63:1). And that is true, O Lord; I do indeed pine for you. I seek you everywhere: in my wife, in my children, in your Church, in the Scriptures, in the woods. I sit in my yard among the spruce and oaks and listen to the birds and watch the rabbits, and I think: These trees and these creatures give you glory. You know, O Lord, which way that robin will fly, and you know when that oak tree will sprout full leaf.

If you know such things, Lord, then you must know me. Yet, I feel you know me not. I reach for you, and you withdraw. I call to you, and I hear nothing. If you know me, why then don't you acknowledge me? I feel as though you are passing by, not stopping for me at all.

Is my unlikeness the cause of your silence? You created me, O God, in your likeness. But have my sins, which distort your image like a cracked mirror, driven me to the land of unlikeness? O God, change me from unlikeness to likeness, from a mirror cracked to a mirror whole, from imagelessness to image. Scrape the rust of sin from me that I may gleam like newly wrought iron. Do not allow my foolishness to ruin that which you proclaimed good. Do not banish me to an alien land! Has your image in me been lost by my sin, or is your image yet there, and only your likeness has faded away? As a dog leaps for joy at its master's return, so I will sing for joy at the sight of your face.

Yes, it is your face I seek; hide not your face! "Happy the people who know the festal shout, who walk, O LORD, in the light of your countenance" (Ps 89:15). "Make his face to shine upon us" (Ps 67:1). But when all my seeking comes to naught, I grow so disheartened that I can hardly believe that I believe in you at all, and I loathe myself all the more! If you do not illumine my life with the light of your face, I shall be one as in the tomb.

Answer me, my God! Will the voice that shatters the cedars of Lebanon not whisper to my heart? What must I do? Where must I travel? Whom must I seek to hear your voice? If I climb the mountain, you are there. If I descend into the cave, you are there. But if you are with me, why am I not with you? What comes between us? Is it my sins, which are always before me? And if this be so, where is he who bore the sins of the world, he who was nailed to the tree? Wash me clean! Deliver me from the land of unlikeness!

I mean no impudence. I am consumed with longing, and so I dare. Do not chastise my boldness, nor hold me in contempt. But I am worn out with longing, and I grow tired of talking to the wall. Have mercy on your servant, and help my unbelief.

❦

"Give me the wisdom that sits by your throne, and do not reject me from among your servants" (Wis 9:4). If I am to grow in your likeness, then Wisdom and I must kiss, for I am lacking in comprehension and wanting in your ways. For Wisdom, Sophia, was with you when you made the world, and she understands what is pleasing to you. Indeed, even if I were to achieve perfection, if Wisdom were not with me, I would be as naught in your eyes.

So make me clay in the hands of the potter Wisdom, and mold me in the shape you desire. Save me, too, from presumption, lest I say to the potter, "Why have you made me thus? You know not what you are doing!"

Rather, instill in me the joy of the touch of your hand, of being formed in your likeness, of forever being shaped in your image.

Yet, I wonder: When your hand forms and molds me, do your hands turn the color of the clay? Are you impervious to touch? When you love, are you affected by the object of your love? When we, your children, love, we are indeed affected by the beloved just as we affect the beloved. But "you are the same, and your years have no end" (Ps 102:27), and thus this is not so. How then can you know me? Nothing is added to you by my loving you, nor is anything taken away from you if I should fall from your sight.

But such is Wisdom, who attends your throne! For blessedness of soul lies not in moving you, but that I be moved by you, by your love, which is to say your hand molding me, and your face shining upon me. So do not simply form me with your hand, but squish the clay between your fingers that I may ooze from every portion of your hand. Allow the clay to be as mush in your hand so that I may swirl around you, ever ready to conform to the shape of your desire.

And thus we shall be one, as you and the Word and the Holy Spirit are one. That is the consummation of life, the perfection, the peace: that your hand, so imbedded in the clay, is indistinguishable from the form of the clay. Give me Wisdom that I might not shrink from your hand!

Such is mercy, the fruit of Wisdom: that though I seek to slip from your hand, you sustain me anyhow. Though we are created by you for you, we desire to create ourselves. And in your mercy you place us back into your hands. For what mother says to her babe, "I know you not?" Or what father says to his child, "Be gone from me?"

In time my name will be forgotten and no one will remember my deeds. But Wisdom, who penetrates and pervades all things, will penetrate my soul, and thus will the Lord remember my name. For not one who dwells with Wisdom will the Lord not love. Then what care I for earthly fame?

✖

"O taste and see the goodness of the LORD," says the psalm (34:8). O Lord, O Wisdom, I do desire to taste you. For tasting you is better than knowing you, and tasting you is better than reading about you. What lover desires only a letter from his beloved?

> Oh, may your breasts be like clusters of the
> > vine
> > And the scent of your breath like apples,
> And your kisses like the best wine
> > that goes down smoothly,
> > gliding over lips and teeth.
> I am my beloved's. (Song 7:8–10)

Rather, I want to feel you and be with you, just as I desire to make love to my wife and feel her skin next to mine. And just as I hand myself over to my wife in complete naked trust, so I commend myself to you in stark raw faith.

But how weak is my faith! It matches not even the trust in my wife. Does this displease you? Does this make me less in your eyes? Make my love for you match my love for my wife. Help me to love that which I cannot see!

Or can I? Are you not in her, and is she not your image? The gift of my wife, then, is the gift of yourself. And when she and I make love, when we are buried deep within one another, am I not loving you as well?

I shall pluck, then, the clusters of Wisdom and stuff them into my mouth! I will slurp the wine that flows off her lips and teeth! For then I will certainly taste you, feel you, smell you. I will know you.

For I belong to you! You created me to be with you, and you desire me not to be separated from you. Who desires to be separated from his beloved?

And yet...you have neither form nor substance. I can wrap my wife in my arms, and she and I can entwine our limbs. That is, I can apprehend her. But you, O Wisdom, O Lord, are "more mobile than any motion" (Wis 7:24). How, then, am I to see your face except in her face? I cannot apprehend as I desire, so I will desire what I can apprehend.

Your servant Boethius once said, "We ought to try to believe in a thing as it actually is." You, O Lord, are I AM WHO AM. How can I believe in something like that? But Jesus the Christ, your Son, said, "Whoever has seen me has seen the Father" (John 14:9), and so I will *believe* through the church fathers who saw the apostles who saw him, but I will *love* you through the image of my wife and sons and neighbor whom I see.

You, then, O Wisdom, O Lord God, are made manifest; you are epiphany. You are so, through your creation. But unlike your creation, you have neither beginning nor end. You are the burning bush, burning yet unconsumed. You live in your creation, but you are not bound by it. You live in your image called wife, child, and neighbor, but you are not bound by them.

Do I not kiss my wife's mouth? Do I not stroke my son's hair? Do I not shake my neighbor's hand? Allow me always, then my God, to kiss and stroke and shake you! For you are the Word, but you are not mere letters or sound. For you are the Father, but a Father who runs toward his wayward children. For you are Breath, but sweet as the vine. So allow me to taste you and feel you! You know I want to love you! For a love far distant soon grows dry and brittle. O Lord God, "let me see your face, let me hear your voice, for your voice is sweet and your face is lovely" (Song 2:14).

Notes

Chapter 1

1. Bernard of Clairvaux, *Sermons on Conversion*, trans. Marie-Bernard Said (Kalamazoo, MI: Cistercian Publications, 1981), 61.

2. Halcyon Backhouse, ed., *The Song of Songs: Selections from the Sermons of St. Bernard of Clairvaux* (London: Hodder and Stoughton, 1990), 136.

3. Rachel Fulton, "Taste and See that the Lord is Sweet (Ps 33:9): The Flavor of God in the Monastic West," *Journal of Religion* 86 (2006), 181.

4. William of St. Thierry, *Exposition on the Song of Songs*, trans. Mother Columba Hart (Kalamazoo, MI: Cistercian Publications, 1968), 80.

5. John Cassian, *The Conferences*, trans. Boniface Ramsey (New York: Paulist Press, 1997), 744.

Chapter 3

1. Jacques Dupuis, *Christianity and the Religions: From Confrontation to Dialogue* (Maryknoll, NY: Orbis Books, 2002), 42.

2. Jacques Dupuis, *Who Do You Say I Am?* (Maryknoll, NY: Orbis Books, 2002), 162.

Chapter 4

1. Joseph Klausner, *Jesus of Nazareth: His Life, Time and Teaching* (New York: Macmillan, 1929), 294.

2. John R. Donahue and Daniel Harrington, *The Gospel of Mark*, Sacra Pagina, vol. 2 (Collegeville, MN: Liturgical Press, 2002), 234.

3. Joel Marcus, *Mark 1–8*, Anchor Bible Series, vol. 27 (New York: Doubleday, 2000), 465.

4. Robert H. Gundry, *Mark: A Commentary of His Apology for the Cross* (Grand Rapids, MI: Eerdmans Publishing Co., 1993), 375.

Chapter 5

1. William R. Herzog II, *Parables as Subversive Speech: Jesus as Pedagogue of the Oppressed* (Louisville, KY: Westminster / John Knox Press, 1994), 188.

2. Joachim Jeremias, *Rediscovering the Parables* (New York: Charles Scribners, 1966), 114.

3. F. Gerald Downing, "Ambiguity of 'The Pharisee and the Tax Collector'" *CBQ* 54 (1992), 83. I am not convinced of this argument, however. If the first hearers of the parable were Gentile,

Downing might have a case. Jews, not Gentiles, though, were most likely the first hearers of the parable. Though these Jewish hearers might balk at the tax collector's plea due to his inability to provide restitution, those same Jewish hearers would probably nod in approval of the *piety* of the tax collector, that is, the posture, gestures, and words the man made and spoke.

4. Bernard Brandon Scott, *Hear Then the Parable* (Minneapolis: Fortress Press, 1989), 97.

5. Joseph A. Fitzmyer, *The Gospel According to Luke*, Anchor Bible Series (Garden City, NY: Doubleday, 1981), 1184. "For in this sense this passage joins those of chapter 15 as one of the great Lucan parables of mercy."

Chapter 6

1. Walter M. Abbott, ed., *Documents of Vatican II* (New York: America Press, 1966), 715.

2. Response to a written question at the conclusion of his address to the USCCB at the Basilica of the National Shrine of the Immaculate Conception, crypt church, Washington, DC, April 16, 2008.

3. *Liturgy of the Hours*, vol. 2 (New York: Catholic Book Publishing Company, 1976), 873.

4. *Liturgy of the Hours*, vol. 3 (New York: Catholic Book Publishing Company, 1976), 412.

5. Thomas Merton, *The Inner Experience* (San

Francisco: Harper Collins, 2004), 38–39.

6. Robert Daly, "Images of God and the Imitation of God: Problems of Atonement," *Theological Studies* 68 (2007), 41.

7. Charles Taylor, *A Secular Age* (Cambridge, MA: Harvard University Press, 2007), 262.

Chapter 8

1. John Climacus, *The Ladder of Divine Ascent*, trans. Colm Luibheid and Norman Russell (Mahwah, NJ: Paulist Press, 1982), 224.

2. Climacus, 228.

Chapter 9

1. Paul Evdokimov, *Ages of the Spiritual Life*, trans. Michael Plekon and Alexis Vinogradov (Crestwood, NY: St. Vladimir's Seminary Press, 1998), 170.

Chapter 10

1. Alexander Schmemann, *The Journals of Alexander Schmemann* (Crestwood, NY: St. Vladimir Seminary Press, 2000), 10.

2. Nicodemos of the Holy Mountain, *Handbook of Spiritual Counsel*, trans. Peter A. Chamberas (Mahwah, NJ: Paulist Press, 1989), 159.

3. *The Cloud of Unknowing*, trans. William Johnston (New York: Doubleday, 1973), 134–35.
4. Nicodemos of the Holy Mountain, 167.

Chapter 11

1. John Climacus, 269.
2. Jim Forest, *Praying with Icons* (Maryknoll, NY: Orbis Books, 1997), 45.
3. John Climacus, 269.

Chapter 12

1. Thomas Merton, *The Climate of Monastic Prayer* (Kalamazoo, MI: Cistercian Publications, 1969), 122.
2. Evagrius Ponticus, *The Praktikos & Chapters on Prayer*, trans. John Eudes Bamberger (Kalamazoo, MI: Cistercian Publications, 1981), 74.
3. *Cloud of Unknowing*, 50.
4. Thomas Merton, *Prayer and Self-Growth*. Cassette tape A2400 (Kansas City, MO: Credence Communications), 1994.

Chapter 13

1. Paul Evdokimov, 58.
2. Raymond E. Brown, *An Introduction to New*

Testament Christology (Mahwah, NJ: Paulist Press, 1994), 151.

3. Paul Evdokimov, 107.

Chapter 15

1. Bernard of Clairvaux, *Talks on the Song of Songs*, trans. Bernard Bangley (Brewster, MA: Paraclete Press, 2002), 145.

2. William of St. Thierry, *Exposition on the Song of Songs*, trans. Mother Columba Hart (Kalamazoo, MI: Cistercian Publications, 1968), 64.

3. David Bell, *The Image and Likeness: The Augustinian Spirituality of William of St. Thierry* (Kalamazoo, MI: Cistercian Publications, 1984), 115.

4. William of St. Thierry, *The Golden Epistle*, trans. Theodore Berkeley (Kalamazoo, MI: Cistercian Publications, 1980), 95.

5. William of St. Thierry, *The Golden Epistle*, 94.

6. William of St. Thierry, *Mirror of Faith*, trans. Thomas X. Davis (Kalamazoo, MI: Cistercian Publications, 1979), 19.

7. Augustine, *De Trinitate*, trans. Edmund Hill (New York: New City Press, 1991), 231.

Chapter 16

1. Edward Schillebeeckx, *Church: The Human Story of God* (New York: Crossroad, 1993), 155.

Chapter 17

1. William of St. Thierry, *The Mirror of Faith*, trans. Thomas X. Davis (Kalamazoo, MI: Cistercian Publications, 1979), 3.

2. Luke Timothy Johnson, *The Living Gospel* (New York: Continuum, 2005), 195.